Sx3/230.

£3·25.

JMSurrew.
·· 1986·

The Joy of All Creation

An Anglican Meditation on the Place of Mary

A. M. ALLCHIN

Foreword by
Edward Yarnold, s.j.

Darton, Longman and Todd
London

1984

First published in 1984 by
Darton, Longman and Todd Ltd
89 Lillie Road, London SW6 1UD

© 1984 A. M. Allchin

ISBN 0 232 51611 1

British Library Cataloguing in Publication Data

Allchin, A. M.
  The joy of all creation.
  1. Mary, *Mother of Jesus Christ*—Theology
  2. Church of England—Doctrines
  I. Title.
  232.91   BT610

  ISBN 0–232–51611–1

Phototypeset by Input Typesetting Ltd, London SW19 8DR
Printed in Great Britain by Anchor Brendon Ltd
Tiptree, Essex

For the Guardians and the
Administrator of the Shrine
of Our Lady
of Walsingham
and in grateful memory
of Demetrios Koutroubis
21 July 1921–1 March 1983

Blessed she by all creation
Who brought forth the world's salvation

Contents

Acknowledgements

Excerpts from *Four Quartets* by T. S. Eliot are reprinted by permission of Faber and Faber Ltd and Harcourt Brace Jovanovich Inc; copyright 1943 by T. S. Eliot; renewed 1971 by Esme Valerie Eliot. Excerpts from *Collected Poems* by Edwin Muir are reprinted by permission of Faber and Faber Ltd and Oxford University Press Inc, New York; copyright © 1960 by Willa Muir. The devotion by Thomas Traherne printed on pp. 86–7 is reproduced by courtesy of the Curators of the Bodleian Library, Oxford (MS. Eng. th. e 51).

The author is deeply grateful to the American Region of The Society of Mary, and to a number of friends in Texas, for generous assistance in the publication of this work.

Foreword

Having been associated with Donald Allchin over the past twenty years in a number of ecumenical endeavours, often in connection with the Ecumenical Society of the Blessed Virgin Mary, it has given me great pleasure to be asked to contribute this foreword to his Anglican vision of Mary as the Joy of Creation.

'Modern Anglican theology', wrote a former Archbishop of Canterbury,[1] 'owes many of its characteristics to the central place held within it by the Incarnation.' Canon Allchin sees in the Anglican writers he studies the truths of the Incarnation and the Church coming together in the person of Mary. In all three areas of doctrine there is exemplified the sacramental principle that God comes to his people through the medium of created things.

It has been one of the insights of recent ecumenical theology that the unity of Christians to which Christ calls us is not a blend in which all differentiation is lost, but a skein in which the different traditions retain their distinct and complementary identity. Pope Paul VI spoke of 'the living beauty of the bride of Christ, the Church, wrapped in her many-coloured garment, clothed, we mean, in a legitimate pluralism of traditional expressions'.[2] As Canon Allchin shows, the Anglican thread that is woven into this particoloured Christian understanding of our Lady has two special qualities: it prefers poetic imagery to abstract speculation, and it expresses joy.

For Lancelot Andrewes in the seventeenth century, Mary is the Land of Promise, the good earth which brings forth the Saviour. For the poet Henry Vaughan she is 'the true love's knot', by whom 'God is made our ally'; 'the glad world's blessed maid,/Whose beauty brought life to thy house'. Jeremy Taylor sees the 'two glories' of mother and maid meeting in her like the sun and the moon; in the fullness of her joy 'she was carried like a full vessel', with 'a quietness symbolical to the holy guest of her spotless womb'. In her 'quiet and silent piety' the Holy Ghost descended on her 'like rain into a fleece of wool'. Her reticence about the Annunciation, even to Joseph, is 'like rain falling in uninhabited valleys, where no eye observes the showers; yet the valleys laugh and sing to God in their refreshment without a witness'. Taylor muses on the 'collision of joys' at the Visitation, when 'two mothers of two great princes meet'. For Mark Frank 'the glorious Virgin's lap' is 'the shrine and altar . . . where the Saviour of the world is laid to be adored and worshipped'. Thomas Traherne's litany of praise of God for the Blessed Virgin speaks of her as 'nearest unto Thee, in the Throne of God. . . Tabernacle of the most glorious Trinity. . . The most Illustrious Light in the Church, Wearing over all her Beauties the veil of Humility'.

In the nineteenth century, Anglican writing on Mary is less exuberant, but no less joyous. Addressing the 'Virgin-born', Bishop Reginald Heber exclaims, 'Blessed was the parent's eye/ That watched thy slumbering infancy'. For John Keble the 'Sacramental Touch of the Church' is 'the Touch of Christ', in which Mary is 'especially instrumental' and 'the most glorious instance'. Keble was, however, dissuaded from publishing the poem in which he allowed invocation directed towards the Blessed Virgin: 'So unforbidden may we speak/ An Ave to Christ's Mother meek;/ (As children with 'good morrow' come/ To elders in some happy home).'

Among the writers of our own century, Canon Allchin limits his attention to the poets. Describing a stained glass window, the Welsh poet Euros Bowen speaks of Mary's form appearing 'like the brightest of flowers . . . a gentle virgin, like a heaven of snow. . ./ Fair swirling waters at Aberglasyn,/ Bilberries trailing their myrrh on the Berwyns'. 'The Virgin is a cup, a grail for the blood of the Spirit.' T. S. Eliot sees no end to the tragedies of the sea, 'Only the hardly, barely prayable/ Prayer of the one Annunciation'. Mary is the 'Lady, whose shrine stands on the promontory', on the boundary between earth and heaven.

The word to sum up these writers' attitude to Mary is 'love'. Members of the Roman Catholic communion, to which I belong, will find their devotion to Mary enriched by Canon Allchin's study.

Edward Yarnold s.j.

NOTES
[1]A. M. Ramsey, *From Gore to Temple*, London (1960), p. 27.
[2]*Acta Apostolicae Sedis*, 64 (1972), pp. 197–8.

Preface

This book began to be written almost fifteen years ago. In its early stages it owed much to an invitation to lecture on the Anglican approach to Mariology in the ecumenical section of the Institut Catholique in Paris. I am grateful for the opportunity which was then given me to think and read further on this subject. After many delays, the book was at last finished under the hospitable roof of the Abbey of Ste Marie du Mont in northern France, a house, like all Cistercian monasteries, dedicated to our Lady. The prayers and friendship of the brethren did much to make its conclusion possible.

But though being begun and ended in France, the book itself is very English and very Anglican. It contains a study of a forgotten strand in the history of Anglican thought and devotion. Among the writers considered in it, only Euros Bowen and Edwin Muir are not English, and only Edwin Muir is not Anglican; and they both come from the British Isles. Because the intellectual history of Anglicanism is very little known even to Anglicans, I have provided at the end a kind of dramatis personae, a list of the principal writers involved, with an indication of their dates and character, in order to introduce others to some of the ramifications of our family tree.

I hope in this way to facilitate the use of the book for a variety of readers from a variety of backgrounds; ordinary worshippers who may be interested to learn a little more of what lies behind hymns they sing and prayers they say; readers of English literature who may be glad to discover something of the thinking which informs the prose of Thomas Traherne or the poetry of T. S. Eliot; Christians of various denominations who, in a time of universal convergence, may wish to know more about a tradition which for 400 years has tried to take a mediating position between the separated Churches, and sought to find points of reconciliation in situations of controversy. One of the reasons why the seventeenth-century section bulks large is that the works of most of the writers studied there are almost wholly unobtainable for the great majority of readers. It has been necessary to quote at length to give something of their flavour as well as their content. But Mark Frank's understanding of joy is a thing so splendid in itself as to need no further justification. Many friends have helped, directly and indirectly, in the writing of this book. One in particular I must mention, the late Demetrios Koutroubis of Athens, theologian, whose body now lies buried at North Barsham, close to our Lady's shrine at Walsingham, a place which he very dearly loved.

In the late 1960s when the book was being begun, the themes which it tackles seemed decidedly outlandish. In the years which have passed since then, the theological climate has changed greatly. To speak now of the place of the body in the Christian scheme of things, of the nature of the joy which should inform Christian worship, and of the role of Mary in the drama of salvation, is less unexpected than it was in the late 1960s. The steadily increasing interest in prayer and spirituality, the growing sense that we need to understand more of our poetic and intuitive capacities as well as our strictly rational ones, the new concern for the appreciation of the hidden, feminine element in the Christian tradition, all these things relate to the themes considered in this book. It is my hope that these pages may be of help in bringing old and new light to bear on the consideration of some of the urgent questions with which our times confront us.

A. M. ALLCHIN

Introduction

It is of the very nature of the Christian gospel, and indeed of all Christian praying and thinking, that it is at once particular, concerned with this place and this time, anchored in the specificity of things, and at the same moment full of eternity and mysteriousness. It is a meeting place where something of earth encounters something of heaven. We shall not understand it unless we see both sides of the antinomy; that it is precisely not abstract and generalized, but specific and only thus universal.

This sacramental or symbolic quality in Christian thinking and living has tended to be lost to sight in recent centuries in the development of an intellectualized theology itself deeply influenced by the intellectual and spiritual development of the West since the Renaissance and the Reformation. This whole tendency has made for a separation between spirit and matter, mind and body, so that the body and the material world have become increasingly divorced from the realm of mind and spirit, and have been sometimes ignored and despised, and sometimes cultivated and worshipped as ends in themselves. In the last hundred years especially we have sought to preserve an inner world of meaning and subjectivity, over against the threat of an outer world of vast, impersonal and mechanistic realities.

Everywhere at the present time there is a sense that this development has run its course; people are seeking to find new ways to put together worlds which have been too long separated. Indeed the very facts of our time, inner and outer alike, are forcing us to

1

the discovery of a new wisdom. One of the central areas in this new discovery is the reaffirmation of the place of the body in our life as human beings. In medicine and psychology, in philosophy and theology alike, it is seen with new force that man is a unity, not mind and matter, not soul and body, as two distinct entities, but a single reality of life, a human person in whom soul and body are at one. Human life, in its most 'spiritual', its most personal aspects, is lived in and through the body, and not apart from it. Knowing is a bodily function; not only in that union of man and woman in mutual giving, which in Hebrew was called knowledge, but in all forms of knowing, which are in some degree personal and embodied. And though we cannot dispense with reason and consciousness, knowledge is something more than the conscious and rational activity of the mind alone. We know with the whole of ourselves.

This is pre-eminently true of the knowledge of God. If we can know God at all, it is with a knowledge in which the body and the senses participate. If we are to know the divine, our ears and eyes no less than our hearts and minds must be made apt to the perception of heavenly realities. There are many stirrings of this insight at the present time, and it is one of the places in which the voice of William Blake sounds with a particular and prophetic urgency. But Blake is not alone among the thinkers and seers of the first part of the nineteenth century to be aware of the deeper currents of the human spirit in his time. Coleridge in his own very different way, is being revealed as a thinker of no less prophetic power. And one of the greatest of Anglican theologians of the nineteenth century, one who combined the role of theologian and natural scientist, wedded meticulous scholarship to visionary insight, F. J. A. Hort, already in the mid-nineteenth century was pointing to him in this connection. In his remarkable but little known essay on Coleridge of 1856, Hort writes:

Philosophy has denied that it has anything to do with the know-ledge of God, and is now being rapidly swallowed up by positivism and science militant, and ancient experience tells us of a yet lower deep. Yet when we shall seem to lie at the lowest point, we may perhaps be near the very highest *and the senses them-*

2

selves may become the very instruments of our deliverance. Then philosophy may begin afresh once more, as from its Ionic cradle; and the spirit of Coleridge, which seemed to be aimlessly stooping over a buried past, will be found rich in prophecy for a living future.[1]

It will be part of the purpose of this book to furnish an indirect commentary on this packed and hermetic statement. It need hardly be said that when Hort speaks here of 'science militant', he is not arguing against the natural sciences in themselves. Had he not thought their development essential for the future of mankind he would hardly have devoted so much of his own time to the study of them. Rather he is speaking of a militant 'scientism', which by denying the necessity of other forms of knowing and thinking than those employed in the investigation of material phenomena, or by seeking to assimilate all such other forms to itself, effectively destroys the very basis upon which it operates. Again, the reference to the pre-Socratic philosophers, while it may strike us as in a way prophetic of the interest which they have aroused in the present century, ought not to engage our attention too exclusively. What is essential is the conviction of Coleridge, that the whole content of a long process of development may be given in principle in its initial instant, and that the development of human knowledge and understanding is more like the unfolding and articulation of a single infinitely rich moment of vision, than a simple linear progression from one phase to another. In both cases, as Hort points out, it will be through the senses themselves that we may find our liberation, may become free again to live in a world which is not ultimately subject to meaninglessness and death.

For the body and the senses cannot be ignored in any serious reflection on the Christian mystery. The idea of incarnation indeed focuses our attention upon them from the outset. An older theologian than Hort, and a near contemporary of Blake, one of the few genuinely theological spirits in an age of little vision in the Church, wrote:

The Gospel commenced in an accommodation to man's animal exigencies which was as admirable as it was gracious. . . The Incarnation of the co-eternal Son, through which St John was

3

enabled to declare what he and his fellow-Apostles 'had seen with their eyes, what they had looked upon and their hands had handled, of the Word of Life,' was, in the first instance, so to consult human nature in its animal and sensitive capacity, as to give the strongest pledge that a dispensation thus introduced would, in every subordinate provision, manifest the same spirit and operate on the same principle.[2]

God's way of acting is all of a piece. He wills to be incarnate now no less than then. The incarnation of the co-eternal Son cannot be an isolated wonder. However we interpret its uniqueness, and all Christian tradition insists that in some sense it is unique, we cannot think of it as something of the past. It is, as Alexander Knox says, the source of a permanent admiration.

Here already the place of Mary within the Christian dispensation is clearly coming into view. God enters into the material world. He is present at the roots of man's affective, natural, bodily life. The fullness of the deity is revealed not only in the mind and speech of Jesus, but in his body, that which he took from us, that in which he is most at one with us. The most basic of human experiences, of needs and satisfactions, fulfilments and anxieties are the soil in which the divine is revealed and grows. Every human act, rooted in the material, animal order, for man is part of the material world and shares much with the animal creation, can yet become fully human, in becoming free and consciously realized, can indeed be known as a gift, discovered as a response of thanks to God, can be divine. Grace shines through, illuminates and transfigures the natural order in its totality, shows that it has a wholly unsuspected goal and destiny; for God has entered into the very processes of birth.

Here in classical Christian faith there is a very great affirmation of the goodness of the human, despite all its empirical disorder and decay. The human is capable of the divine. Through the gift of God, the divine life is rooted in the human, the human in the divine. And here precisely is the cause of great joy and amazement. For precisely in 'man's animal exigencies' the ultimate glory is revealed, just where we had least expected it. Hence everywhere in the Christian world where she is known, Mary's name is associated with joy. She is the joy of joys, the cause of our joy, the joy of all creation. Latin, Greek, Russian, Syriac all proclaim the same thing. In her there is a meeting of opposites, of God and man, of flesh and spirit, of time and eternity, which causes an explosion of joy, of a kind of ecstasy. It is the joy which is known in human life, 'when the opposites come together, and the genuinely new is born'.[3]

Christianity says much about suffering and sorrow, pain and grief, and the way forward through death to life, through separation to a final and ultimate unity. In a world such as ours it would not be of much use, if it were unable to confront these realities of suffering and separation. But this is not all that it has to say. The gospel can also speak of a joy and innocence, which if it is known fleetingly in this world is yet a true element in man's experience. If at first we might be tempted merely to juxtapose these two visions, the vision of innocence and life, the vision of death and resurrection, deeper reflection will show that the two are most intimately connected, and that in this world the former is strangely dependent on the latter. Only in the light of the triumph of the cross can this world be seen as again touched by the divine glory. It is from the cross that joy has come into the world.

The great mosaic in the church of the Holy Wisdom in Istanbul speaks eloquently of this fact. It presents the figure of Christ, between that of the Baptist and the Virgin Mother. On the one side is the prophet, the face furrowed with grief, with the sorrow of this world, its experience of frustration, of not fulfilling the purpose for which it was created, yet looking with a hope, hardly won, towards the way of repentance, the way of newness of life. On the other side is the figure of Mary, in the purity and transparence of her human beauty, the transfiguration of that vision of the perfection of man's body which characterized ancient Greece. Both things are true, and both meet in the grave yet radiant majesty of the central figure of the Christ.

The same thing is to be seen again in the same city, once the queen of cities, the particular heritage of the Queen of heaven, in the mosaics of the church of Our Saviour in Chora. Here in the narthex and exonarthex are a whole series of brilliant and delicate representations of the birth and childhood of Mary, and of the

5

birth and childhood of Jesus. They are a celebration of human love and tenderness, of the care of parents for their children, of the joy of children in the security of their parents' love, and they formed the ground, the basis for the further development of the mystery of man's salvation which would have been unfolded in the mosaics of the central space of the church, but which are no longer in existence. Baptism, transfiguration, crucifixion, resurrection and ascension, all these things are rooted in the coming together of Joachim and Anna, or in the nurture of the infant Jesus. To stop at these first images would be to perceive only a part of the truth; to seek to omit them would be to misconceive the greater realities to which they lead on.

It has not been customary to speak in this way in theology, to make such use of mosaic and poetry as we shall do in this study. Can we take such things 'seriously' in a serious context? Is the knowing of an artist or a poet, serious knowing; can it tell us the truth, or is it mere imaginative fancy? It will be clear that for us, the power of vision, physical and imaginative, no less than intellectual, has its part to play in the work of theology. Not that the imagination is in some special way a divine faculty, or that it can not be deceived. It shares with the reason man's condition of fallenness, and it can be deceitful in its own fashion. But if the work of theology is to have at its centre the texts of the Bible and the liturgy, then we must allow that the image will have a certain priority over the concept, for these texts are for the most part imagist rather than conceptual. This does not mean that conceptual thinking is not necessary, or that it can be simply replaced by a symbolical approach; still less does it mean that we can dispense with clarity and precision. The work of theology has need of all the clarity and accuracy which we can bring into it. But we shall recognize that in approach to the truth of God something more than simple accuracy is required. In some sense it is images and symbols which come first. It is concepts which elucidate and clarify them.

Indeed we shall be led in the course of this study to affirm that in our own century it has been the poets rather than the professional teachers of theology who have often fulfilled the true theological function, of speaking of the divine revealed in the human, of the human taken into the divine, of declaring the true nature of man's life as sacramental, full of mysteriousness, a potentiality which it can never fully contain or express. 'They declare, with a perpetual insistence, the mysteriousness of our present being . . . they take the side of faith and patience against the attractions of completeness and security and achievement and repose.'[4]

The words quoted speak, in their original context, of sacraments not of poets. Yet they are true of both, and are followed by a remarkable tribute from a late nineteenth-century theologian to an early nineteenth-century poet, in which the hierarchical order in the Church – for the writer, Francis Paget, was already a regius professor and later became a dean and a bishop – pays due respect to the prophetic or charismatic order. They are words which point to truths which the experience of our own century has only rendered more clear and evident.

It is given sometimes to a poet to sink a shaft, as it were, into the very depths of the inner life: to penetrate its secret treasuries, and to return, Prometheus-like, with a gift of fire and of light to men. The venturesome words that record such a moment of penetration and insight never lose their power; they seem to have caught something of the everlasting freshness of that world of which they speak: and one man after another may find in them, at some time of need or gladness or awakening, the utterance of thoughts which else he might have been too shy or too faint-hearted to acknowledge even to himself. There is such a splendid venture of courage for the truth's sake in those lines of Wordsworth which surely no familiarity can deprive of their claim to reverence and gratitude; the lines in which he tells us of his thankfulness

. . . for those obstinate questionings
Of sense and outward things,
   Fallings from us, vanishings;
   Blank misgivings of a creature
Moving about in worlds not realised,
High instincts before which our mortal nature
Did tremble like a guilty thing surprised.
   . . . those first affections,

Those shadowy recollections,
Which, be they what they may,
Are yet the fountain-light of all our day,
Are yet a master-light of all our seeing;
  Uphold us, cherish, and have power to make
Our noisy years seem moments in the being
  Of the eternal silence . . .'[5]

Very characteristically Wordsworth speaks here of two distinct yet closely connected things. There are 'the first affections, the shadowy recollections', the memory from before consciousness, the haunting sense of eternity and wholeness perceived in childhood, on the one side; and on the other side, there are the questionings, the misgivings of the adult world, the sense of fear, indeed the guilt before the infinite, which can open up within the fabric of our daily lives, and suddenly bestow on them an unexpected sense and meaning. These moments, these recollections, though in the deepest sense spiritual, indeed divine, are never, in Wordsworth, disincarnate or generalized. They are felt through the senses, known through sight and smell, through hearing and touch, rooted in the life of the body.[6] 'The moments of such visitation are', Paget continues, 'the supreme opportunities of a human soul, the crises of its tragedy. . . We rise and we live and grow and see by the right understanding and employment of such moments. . .', for in them we can find 'the disclosure, the assertion, the stepping forward of his presence who alone sustains our life, our thought, our love'.[7]

If, as Christian faith has always affirmed, it is in the man Jesus of Nazareth that we find the supreme disclosure, assertion, stepping forward of him who alone sustains our life, our thought, our love, then the person of the woman who was his mother, out of whom, bodily, he came cannot but be a central theme of Christian reflection.

But how are we to approach this subject of the place and role of Mary? Even the approach to the question is full of perplexities. On the one hand there is the slender evidence in the New Testament writings, on the other the enormous burgeoning of Christian doctrine and devotion through the centuries. On the one hand there is the silence of Protestantism, sometimes respectful, sometimes indifferent, sometimes hostile, on the other hand the enormous, one might think disproportionate, volume of speculation on the part of the Roman Catholic theologians in the century which preceded Vatican II. Here is a question on which Christians have fought one another and wounded one another. The very terms which they use have been hardened and falsified in the course of a polemic, in which insights given for the healing and restoration of man's life have been used to defend and attack entrenched positions. Here is a question in which thought and feeling are both deeply involved, where no one who begins to reflect finds that he can be altogether neutral. How are Christians from different traditions to break the uneasy silence on this subject which too often reigns between them when they come together?

It might at first sight seem that the obvious place from which to begin is that which all Christians have in common, the Gospels, the New Testament, the Bible as a whole.[8] For a variety of reasons, however, I shall not take that route, not least because this is most evidently one of the places where what Christians see in the biblical texts depends to a large degree on their whole living experience of the Christian reality as it has been mediated to them in the Christian community to which they belong. Instead of beginning with the Gospels I shall begin with tradition, and precisely with the tradition of my own Church, believing that here, as in other places, despite and through all its limitations, Anglicanism can open up a way into the fullness of Christian truth and understanding. I shall begin with our seventeenth-century theologians, men who stood in the life and faith of a community which was conscious both of its continuity with the Church of the centuries before the Reformation, and of its indebtedness to certain of the central affirmations of the Reformers, men who sought to enlarge and deepen that faith and life through a contact with the living tradition of the Fathers of the Church, particularly those who lived before the split between East and West. I follow the method of the Church of England and appeal to the authority of 'the Scriptures as interpreted by the perpetual practice of God's Church', aware that such a large and general criterion will not give quick or easy solutions, but believing that in the end it may prove more satisfactory than other seemingly more attractive alternatives.

I appeal to the seventeenth century not only on account of the largeness of its own understanding of tradition, but also on account of a particular quality of its faith and thought. When in the 1920s one of the greatest poets, and in the older meaning of the word, one of the greatest theologians of our time announced his acceptance of the Christian faith, he did so in a volume called *For Lancelot Andrewes*. The title is not fortuitous. T. S. Eliot found in the sermons of Andrewes, as in the theology of Hooker, in the life of the family at Little Gidding, in the church building of Sir Christopher Wren, signs of a Catholicism which was not ignorant either of the Renaissance or of the Reformation, a tradition which, in that sense had already moved into the modern world and lived on our side of the gulf which separates us from the Middle Ages. It was a Catholicism which had taken humanism and criticism into itself, without being destroyed by them. 'A Catholicism *without* the element of humanism and criticism', Eliot wrote in that book, 'would be a Catholicism of despair.'⁹

Many of Eliot's contemporaries felt that this was the only Catholicism which was available, that the great universal life-giving affirmations of Christian faith could only be made on the basis of the acceptance of a clearly defined external and infallible authority. They sought accordingly to stifle their questions and their scepticism by an appeal to the authority of the central see of Western Christendom. Only since Vatican II has released within the Roman Catholic Church all the forces of a free and questioning Catholicism, has it been possible to measure both the strength and the weakness of that other more despairing and authoritarian version of the Roman tradition to which so many of them adhered. Eliot chose another way. He believed that, for him in England, another form of the Catholic tradition was open, one in which the authority of God's self-disclosure is mediated in a much greater variety of ways. In Andrewes, he wrote, we hear 'the voice of a man . . . who speaks with the old authority and the new culture'. In the theology of his school he found 'a determination to stick to essentials, that awareness of the needs of the times, the desire for clarity and precision in matters of importance, and the indifference to matters indifferent',[10] which seemed to him to indicate a balance of tradition which was necessary in his own times. Still more, he found in the religion of this period something of even greater value to his own faith; a faith which did not so much reject and suppress doubt, as carry its scepticism within itself. Recounting an incident which took place in Cambridge about the time of the publication of *For Lancelot Andrewes*, a friend of Eliot writes: 'As we walked back through the empty courts in the small hours, Eliot made one comment which I always found very helpful in understanding his religious position. There was, he quietly observed, a great difference between the Marxists and himself, not only or merely in the content of his beliefs, but even more in the way in which they were held. "They seem so certain of what they believe. My own beliefs are held with a scepticism which I never even hope to be quite rid of".'[11] The friend who recounts the incident remarks on the light which it throws on Eliot's relationship to the Anglican seventeenth-century poets, to Donne and Herbert in particular, in whom there is the constant interplay between faith and questioning. One might also note here one of the points of affinity between Eliot and his contemporary Charles Williams whose own burning faith contained within itself precisely this vein of questioning and criticism.

Such a faith is in no sense a half-hearted or temporizing thing. Nothing could be clearer than that, both in Eliot's life and in his writing. One is tempted to qualify as heroic his adherence to the strictness of Christian faith in a society and milieu so wholly unsympathetic to it; while his writings, above all the *Four Quartets*, contain an exposition of the depths of the tradition of Christian spirituality and theology which is unequalled in our century. Rather it is a faith which recognizes our hopeless ignorance before the mysteries of God, and does not pretend to find answers when it has not got them. It recognizes at every point 'the mysteriousness of our present being'. It 'takes the side of faith and patience against the attractions of completeness and security and achievement and repose'. It is a factor in the Anglican tradition which makes for a certain tentativeness and humility before the affirmations of theology and which corresponds very closely to the apophatic elements, the awe and the reserve, which characterize the teaching

11

of the great Fathers of East and West alike. This characteristic does not imply any refusal of knowledge, any turning away from God's gift of himself. It is rooted rather in an experience of the limitations of man's language and man's concepts, and expresses a humility before the immensity of the divine.

This tradition has, moreover, a further quality which is of equal significance. It recognizes that our approach to God must be complex, multiple, if it is to take in the whole of our being, and in any way correspond to the fullness of God's revelation of himself. God in his approach to us will speak and act in a variety of ways. It will, therefore, distrust any theological system which leans so wholly on transcendence as to emphasize redemption and revelation to the exclusion of creation and nature. It will be as uneasy with any system which tends wholly to immanence, and which loses the specificity of revelation in some general scheme of evolutionary development. In the words of an eminent Anglican theologian of our century, commenting on the theological method of Richard Hooker, 'God as the ultimate reality must be approached by many paths; through the witness of nature and of the religious impulse, as well as through the moral conscience, through each and all of these as well as through the special revelation which he has given us. To each of these too we must allow its own method, only seeking to show how in the end they corroborate one another.'[12] Here is the root of the attempt to differentiate between things essential, and things less essential, between what is of central significance and what of ancillary worth.

It will be our contention that we shall have need of all these qualities in our approach to the vast and sometimes perplexing phenomenon of Marian devotion and reflection, of holy place and pilgrimage, of apparition and locution. We must not, of course, ignore the witness of Scripture, for unless the whole development is in some sense anchored in the heart of the Christian mystery, then it must be condemned as at least irrelevant to the intent of God's act in Jesus Christ. But at the same time we shall not dismiss, as without any value, 'the witness of nature and of the religious impulse', so that while we may scrutinize carefully those places where devotion to the Mother of God seems to bring Christianity most close to other religions, we shall by no means reject them out of hand. The Word of God by whom all things were made, has left his imprint upon all our life and thought, not least upon our strivings after the divine. Above all we shall have need of a respectful agnosticism, neither too hasty to accept or refuse, what at times may seem strange, or even maybe repellent, but rather seeking to see how it relates to the central and amazing affirmation of faith made by all Christians, that God was in Christ and that in man the fullness of the divinity dwelt bodily.

NOTES
1 F. J. A. Hort in 'Coleridge', *Cambridge Essays* (1856)
2 Alexander Knox, *Remains*, vol. i, p. 330
3 Monica Furlong, source unknown
4 Francis Paget, in Charles Gore (ed.), *Lux Mundi* (1889), 'Sacraments', p. 429
5 Ibid., pp. 429–30
6 Cf. Alec King, *Wordsworth and the Artist's Vision: an Essay in Interpretation* (1966)
7 Op. cit., p. 431
8 For an eminently balanced presentation of this subject in the light of Scripture and the early tradition of the Church, written from an Anglican viewpoint, see John de Satgé, *Mary and the Christian Gospel* (1976)
9 T. S. Eliot, *For Lancelot Andrewes* (1928), p. 140
10 Ibid., p. 17
11 From 'Mistah Kurtz: He Dead' by H. S. Davies, in Allen Tate (ed.), *T. S. Eliot: The Man, his Work* (1967)
12 L. S. Thornton, *Richard Hooker: A Study of his Theology* (1924), p. 104

Part One

The Seventeenth-Century Witness

1

'This We are to Hold': Lancelot Andrewes

'God was in Christ reconciling the world to himself.' The doctrine of the incarnation, as the act of God by which reconciliation is brought about, and man and God are united, was at the heart of the theology of seventeenth-century Anglicanism. Any consideration of the role and person of Mary has to be seen always and only in relation to that great primordial mystery of God's love, and it is in this perspective that the question is viewed by the Anglican writers of this period. 'And for as much as there is no union of God with man without that mean between both which is both, it seemeth requisite·that we first consider how God is in Christ, then how Christ is in us, and how the sacraments do serve to make us partakers of Christ. In other things we may be more brief, but the weight of these requireth largeness.'[1]

With these words Richard Hooker stands back from his detailed examination of the Puritan objections to the Book of Common Prayer and introduces his magisterial discussion of the doctrine of Christ. It is an exposition which recapitulates and reaffirms the teaching of the Fathers and the early Councils, and which established at the foundation of the Anglican theological tradition the inseparable links between the doctrine of Christ, of the Church and the sacraments. It need hardly be said that the whole of this argument in Hooker, and throughout this period, is carried on in the terms which had been employed in the ancient Church; that is to say, in terms of the union of the two natures, human and divine, in the one person of Jesus Christ, the Son of God. These are not necessarily terms which come easily to us. But they represent not only the thought but also the prayer and experience of many centuries. It may well be the task of contemporary theology to see whether with a different approach the same truth may be expressed in other and more accessible phrases. Indeed, if Christendom were united, why should it not be that the Spirit of God would guide us into new formulations no less valid than the old? But we do well to recognize that the traditional categories, stiff though they may sometimes seem to us, express a fullness and balance of faith and insight which is easily betrayed, and that they are therefore not to be lightly laid aside. In seeking to see what they can mean for us in relation to our themes of celebration, of the Mother of the Lord, and the redemption of the body, we may get a new glimpse of the richness of the mystery which they express.

The term *Theotokos*, Mother of God, though defined by the Council of Ephesus, is not used explicitly by Hooker in his treatise *The Laws of Ecclesiastical Polity*. But the faith which the term intended to express and to safeguard is the faith which he is expounding, so that we cannot imagine that he would have rejected it. As to the belief that the life of God touches the whole of us, body and soul alike, there can be no question in his writings. As L. S. Thornton remarks, Hooker's is 'a religion of flesh and blood, of Eucharist and Resurrection', an expression of the tradition which 'comes down to us from the Fourth Gospel, through Irenaeus, Tertullian and the Greek Fathers'.[2] In this connection Hooker's stress upon the true humanity of Christ is particularly important. 'Doth any man doubt', Hooker writes, 'that even from the flesh of Christ our very bodies do receive that life which shall make them glorious at the latter day, and for which they are already accounted parts of his blessed Body? Our corruptible bodies would never live the life they shall live, were it not that here they are joined with his body, which is incorruptible, and that his in ours is a cause of immortality. . . Christ is therefore both as God and as man, that true Vine whereof we both spiritually and corporally are branches.'[3] This union bodily is not to be thought of in crudely physical terms; but it is to be seen as an expression of the faith that even now the healing power of God is at work through our whole nature. This faith is vital for Hooker. And in this work, the sacra-

18

ment of the Eucharist has its part to play. 'In words of endless import', to quote Paget commenting on this section, Hooker affirms ' "there ensueth a kind of transubstantiation in us, a true change of both soul and body, an alteration from death to life." ' As Paget notes, these words rest directly on those of Irenaeus, in the second century: 'As bread from the earth receiving the invocation of God is no longer common bread, but the Eucharist, consisting of two things, an earthly and a heavenly; so our bodies also receiving the Eucharist are no longer corruptible, having the hope of the Resurrection.' 'Alike in us and in the Sacrament,' Paget concludes, 'the powers of the world to come invade the present and already move towards the victory which shall be hereafter.'[4]

We are here already at a stand, not knowing what to feel or think in face of such exalted affirmation about the nature of man, made by Christian thinkers of such widely separated times and places. Certainly, with Jeremy Taylor we may exclaim, 'This great and glorious mystery is the honour and glory of man', or with Lancelot Andrewes, 'This being beyond the rules and reach of all reason is surely matter of astonishment. "This it is, saith St Chrysostom, casteth me into an ecstasy and maketh me imagine of our nature some great matter, I cannot well express what." Thus it is: it is the Lord, let him do what seemeth good in his own eyes.'[5]

The exposition of the Christian faith contained in Lancelot Andrewes's Ninety-six Sermons, preached year by year before the royal court at the great feasts of Christmas, Easter and Whitsun was to become one of the foundation stones of Anglican theology. It constitutes a magisterial unfolding of the richness and coherence of the Christian tradition, demonstrating at every point the relation of one doctrine to another, the necessity of each part to make up the whole. But these intensely theological sermons always have a practical end. They are intended to carry us out beyond ourselves, either into service of our neighbour, or into the love and worship of God. In this as in other things, Andrewes speaks in the manner of the Fathers. His teaching reflects that sober drunkenness of which they speak; by the use of the utmost power of reason going beyond the rules and reach of all reason.

What, in the passage we have quoted above, is it which has moved Andrewes's particular attention? The sermon in which it occurs is based on the text 'For surely it is not with angels that he is concerned but with the descendants of Abraham'. Here is the comparison which the preacher is enforcing. The angels, he declares, 'in everything else, above and before us; in this beneath and behind us. And we unworthy, wretched men that we are, above and before the Angels, the Cherubim, the Seraphim and all the Principalities and Thrones in this dignity.'[6] We shall have later to consider what this comparison of men with angels means in relation to the traditional belief in the incarnation. Here let us simply register the fact that Andrewes is taking up a thread in the tradition which has particular relevance to the person of Christ's Mother, who in the worship of the Orthodox Church is constantly referred to as 'more honourable than the Cherubim, and incomparably more glorious than the Seraphim'. Whatever else these words say, they are evidently an expression of the intimacy with which God and man come together in Christ, and of the infinite distance which has been overcome in order to create that intimacy.

The reference to Mary is made explicitly by Andrewes in a later sermon, on the text of Galatians 4:4, 5. 'When the time was fully come, God sent forth his Son, born of woman, born under the law, to redeem those who were under the law, so that we might receive the adoption of sons.' Here he uses the sermon to expound the union of the two natures in Christ, the coming together of human and divine, of eternity and time.

And so have we here now in one both twain His natures. 'God sent his Son' – there his divine: 'made of a woman' – here his human nature. That, from the bosom of his Father before all worlds; this, from the womb of his mother in the world. So that as from eternity God his Father might say that verse of the Psalm *Filius meus es Tu, hodie genui Te*, 'Thou art my Son, this day have I begotten Thee', so 'in the fullness of time' might the Virgin his Mother no less truly say, *Filius meus es Tu, hodie peperi Te*, 'Thou art my Son, this day have I brought thee into this world.'

And here now at this word 'made of a woman', he beginneth to concern us somewhat. There groweth an alliance between us; for we also are made of a woman. And our hope is, as he will

20

not be confounded, to be counted *inter natos mulierum;* no more will he be, saith the Apostle, to say *in medio fratrum* 'to acknowledge us his brethren'. And so by this time he groweth somewhat near us.[7]

There are two things here which call for our notice. First, the coincidence of the two 'todays', on which Andrewes speaks at length in this and other sermons. In the incarnation, time reaches a certain fullness and, in some way, is taken up into eternity. There is a union here of man's life which passes away, with God's life which does not pass away. Something eternal is realized in time. Time is fulfilled in being transcended. There is an intersection of the timeless with time. And this, which is supremely true of the incarnation itself, is also true of all those moments in which the incarnation is recalled, and made present again. It is true in a particular way of the times when the Church comes together to celebrate and recall these things in worship and thanksgiving. Here is a clue as to the nature of liturgy and of celebration which we shall find worked out in many other places.

The other point which concerns us here, and which leads us further on, is Andrewes's insistence that it is in Christ's sharing our human birth that he comes close to us, is gradually brought into proximity with us, and makes an 'alliance' with us. This is not some diplomatic contract. It is more like an alliance of families, made by marriage. By it, we find that we are 'advanced' beyond anything that we could have imagined. Herein, as Andrewes will underline, is love: Christ's love which draws us up to be where he is.

The same thoughts are to be found in another of the nativity sermons, no. xi, preached on the text from Psalm 85, 'Mercy and Truth are met together, Righteousness and Peace have kissed each other. Truth shall spring out of the earth, and Righteousness shall look down from heaven.'[8] This sermon has lying behind it the first of St Bernard's sermons on the Feast of the Annunciation, which employs the same text. It is interesting as an example of the way in which Andrewes uses not only the earlier Fathers as authoritative spokesmen of the tradition, but is prepared also to advance into the Latin Middle Ages in order to build up his picture of the fullness of the faith. For this is a sermon about fulfilment, about the conjunction of apparent opposites, about a meeting between parties which have been too long separated. 'Truth being now born of our nature, it will never, we may be sure, be against our nature; being come of the earth, it will be true to his own country; being made man, will be for man now all he can.' The link is established, we are all of one party. For Andrewes of course interprets the Psalm verse as a prophecy of the incarnation.

The Truth, this he who declared 'I am the Truth', the earth, what is that but the flesh of man? And as the truth fits his nature, so doth earth man. Of whom God, 'earth thou art' (Gen. 3:19), to whom the Prophet thrice over, 'Earth, hear the word of the Lord' (Jer. 22:20); by whom the wise man, *Quid superbis?* 'Why should the earth be proud' (Ecclus. 10:19) *Germinet terra Salvatorem*, 'Let this earth bring forth a Saviour' – be the *terra promissionis*, the Blessed Virgin, who was in this the land of promise. So was this very place applied by Irenaeus in his time, who touched the Apostles' times; so by Lactantius; so by St Hierom and St Augustine. Those four meet in this sense, as do the four in the text. *Quid est veritas de terra orta? est Christus de faemina natus? Quid est Veritas? Filius Dei. Quid terra? Caro nostra.* 'What the truth? Christ. What the earth? Our flesh.' In those words they find this feast all.'[9]

This interpretation of the Blessed Virgin as 'the good earth', 'the land of promise', which, as we have already suggested, is of great significance, is clearly of some special importance to Andrewes also. He draws out four witnesses from among the Fathers, and insists upon the antiquity of the first of them, as of one who links us with the ages of the apostles. Andrewes has a liking for citing four witnesses from the tradition, as we shall see again. It was the number of the Evangelists, the primary witnesses to the events of the incarnation, it was the number of the first four Ecumenical Councils. It was for him a number which spoke of completeness and assurance.

And in the text four different attributes have met; Peace and Mercy on the one side, Righteousness and Truth on the other. Andrewes pictures the coming together of the apparent opposites

22

in the birth of Christ, who rises out of the good earth, the land of promise, the Blessed Virgin.

And here again he sees a reconciliation of his eternal generation, and this his birth in time. 'For *orta est*, it is double; therefore *de terra* is well added. Another *ortus* he had *de Caelo*; to wit, His heavenly Divine nature which as "the day sprung from on high", and He in regard of it called *oriens* by Zachary in the New Testament (Luke 1:78). But this here is *de terra*; for the word properly signifies "the shooting forth of a sprig out of the ground", and he in regard of this *ortus* called "the Branch" by Zachary in the Old (Zech. 3:8).'

As the sermon continues so we see more of what is involved in the coming together of these four virtues. For Andrewes their conjunction corresponds to a fourfold pattern which can be found in creation as well as in redemption. It speaks of the necessity of completeness if we are to receive God's gift of life. It speaks of a continuing quality which should mark the whole development of the Christian life, personal as well as corporate. There is a fullness which needs to be maintained. 'For as this meeting made Christianity first; so there is nothing mars it, but the breaking it off again; no greater bane to it, than the parting of these.' And he goes on with emphasis:

Set this down then: Christianity is a meeting: one cannot meet, two there must be and they may. But it is not a meeting of two, but of two with two: so, no less than four. . . And as it is a meeting, so a cross meeting, of four virtues that seem to be in a kind of opposition (as hath been noted). No matter for that. They will make the better refraction; the cool of one allay the heat, the moist of one temper the drought of the other. The soft virtues need to be quickened; the more forward to be kept from *altum sapere*. So are the elements of which are our bodies. so are the four winds of which our breath doth consist, which gives us life. And these in the text have an analogy or correspondence with the elements observed by the ancients; truth corresponds with the solid earth, peace with the running streams, mercy with the air we breathe, righteousness with the devouring fire.[10]

Here are themes which will recur in other places in our study of this subject, as we come to reflect further on the way in which the incarnation implies a constant meeting of apparent opposites. For Andrewes this point is of special importance. It is, he maintains, the very essence of heresy to fail to recognize this thing, but instead to take the part for the whole, to accept one truth without its complementary opposing truth. Again he affirms,

> Christianity is a meeting, and to this meeting there go *plia dogmata*, as well as *bona opera*, righteousness as well as truth. Err not this error than to single out any (as it were) in disgrace of the rest; say not, one will serve the turn, what should we do with the rest of the four; . . . The truth is, sever them, and farewell all; take any one from the rest and it is as much as the whole is worth. For (as Bernard well observed) *non sunt virtutes si separentur*, upon their separation they cease to be virtues. . . Entertain them then all four; 1) Hope in Mercy; 2) faith in Truth; 3) fear of Righteousness; 4) love of Peace. . . O how loving a knot! how by all means to be maintained! how great a pity to part it![11]

These are the foundations which Andrewes laid, and the extent to which writers of the later seventeenth century built upon them can be well illustrated from the poem by Henry Vaughan, which might almost be a commentary on these lines,

> Bright Queen of heaven, God's Virgin Spouse
> The glad world's blessed maid,
> Whose beauty brought life to thy house
> And brought us saving aid.
>
> Thou art the true love's knot;
> By thee God is made our ally.
> When our inferior nature, he
> With his doth dignify.
>
> For coalescent by that bond
> We are his body grown
> Nourished with favours from his hand
> Who for our head we own.[12]

But already the poet has taken us further on into the consequences which come from this initial moment of incarnation, on
to the thought of our being united with Christ, as members of his
Body, nourished and built up by his life. These consequences
Andrewes also elaborates in later sermons.

But before we come to them, it is necessary to see a little more
fully what is involved in this doctrine of incarnation, as to the
person of the Mother of the Lord. In view of the fact that in his
sermons Andrewes says quantitatively very little about her, it is
remarkable how much he manages to say in these passages which
we are about to examine from the Ninth Sermon for Christmas
Day, on the text of Isaiah 7:14, 'Behold a virgin shall conceive and
bear a son, and shall call his name Immanuel.' In them he touches
the heart and core of the Church's devotion to Mary.

First we shall see how he stresses that here is something which
goes beyond reason, and yet takes reason up into itself, then how
he underlines that this is something where the power of God and
the faith of man are altogether active in the creation of a new
and paradoxical reality in which the opposites come together, and
reconciliation takes place. And this faith of man, he insists, is not
merely passive, it also contributes to the new thing which comes
to birth.

But I hold ever best to let everything rest upon his own base or
bottom; natural upon reason, supernatural upon faith. And this
is supernatural; in which *tota ratio facti est in potentia facientis*,
'the power of the doer is the reason of the thing done.' God is
the doer, *Cujus dicere est facere*, 'to whom it is as easy to do it
as to say it.' As the Angel concluded, so do I, 'With God is
nothing impossible.' And that of Christ's, 'To faith all things are
possible.' And here are both. And where they meet, they make
no less a miracle than *Mater* and *Virgo*, or *Deus* and *Homo* –
even *fides* and *ratio*. And this, for *Virgo concipiet*.'[13]

From this initial statement, Andrewes goes on to work out what
is involved in this act of conception.

This we are to hold; to conceive is more than to receive. It is so
to receive as to yield somewhat of our own also. A vessel is not

25

said to conceive the liquor that is put into it. Why? Because it yieldeth nothing from itself. The Blessed Virgin is, and therefore is because she did. She did both give and take. Give of her own substance whereof his body was framed; and take or receive power from the Holy Ghost, whereby was supplied the office and the efficacy of the masculine seed. This is *concipiet*.[14]

We are aware by the very formula with which the preacher introduces this discussion, that it is for him a point of some import-ance. 'This we are to hold.' As much as to say, 'this we have received, this we must hand on'. Indeed he quotes from Hilary, Gregory Nazianzen, Gregory the Great, and Bernard to show that this position is not a fancy of his own. Again we see the citing of four witnesses. Furthermore, Andrewes is conscious here of touching upon a point which was contested both by ancient and contemporary heretics. 'And this word is the bane of divers here-sies. That of the Manichee that held, He had no true body. That had been, *virgo decipiet*, not *concipiet*; not – conceive Him, but deceive us. And that of the Valentinian, revived lately in the Ana-baptist, that held He had a true body, but made in Heaven and sent into her. That has been *recipiet* but not *concipiet*, received him she had, conceived him she did not.'[15]

If the former heresy is one which seems unfamiliar to us, the reverse is true of the second even though it is not put in precisely these terms. In schemes of theology which think to safeguard the transcendence and priority of God by denying any true reciprocity on the part of man, we have often heard of an activity of God which comes '*senkrecht von oben*', straight down from above without any contribution whatsoever from man's side, and which therefore can find no place for Christ's Mother either in thought or devotion. The heroic attempts made in the earlier period of Protestant neo-Orthodoxy, in works like Nygren's *Agape and Eros*, to deny the very possibility that men can love God look curiously artificial and unreal when seen in the light of a larger view of Christian thinking and experience. God's love for us is not in word or tongue, but in deed and in truth. It enters into our flesh. To deny the mystery of the transformation which this works in man is not to magnify but to deny the power and reality of this love. As Karl Barth so clearly saw in his later writings, we do not truly exalt God, by seeking to depress man, made in his image. Nor can there be any real relationship of love unless man is able to love in return him by whom he finds himself to be loved.

And this is precisely the point which Andrewes here makes. He does not, as he very properly might have done, draw out from his *concipiet*, the thought about Mary, that she 'gives of her own substance', to the moment of incarnation, so that the divine truly appears in human form, a form with features which he had taken from her. He does not here reflect how much this tells us not only about Mary, but about every man who seeks to make a free response of love to the divine initiative and thereby gives 'of his own substance', that the divine epiphany may take place. Others would do that later. He turns at once to what it says about the love of God, the primal, underlying reality which alone makes sense of, alone makes possible any movement of man's love in response.

> From which his conceiving we may conceive his great love to usward. Love, not only condescending to take our nature upon him, but to take it by the same way and after the same manner that we do, by being conceived. That, and no other better beseeming way. . . . This sure is matter of love; but came there any good to us by it? There did. For our conception being the root as it were, the very groundsill of our nature; that he might go to the root and repair our nature from the very foundation, thither he went; that what had been there defiled and decayed by the first Adam, might by the second be cleaned and set right again.[16]

He not only took our nature, but took it 'by the same way and after the same manner that we do'. He went to its very root, its groundsill. A dimension of the meaning of the incarnation is opened up here, which needs further exploration. We know more clearly than Andrewes did, the links which bind human conception to animal conception; the immensely long processes of evolution which in some way the human embryo recapitulates in the first stages of its development. All this was part of God's patience, all this was in some way assumed. For us, the womb will speak not only of the first and pre-conscious period of the individual's life, but also of all those mysterious areas which lie below and around the centre of our consciousness, areas which are still so little explored, and which still hold for us so much of terror, as well as of amazement. 'Thither he went.' When we look out from the island of consciousness into the surrounding sea of the unconscious, we find, as a twentieth-century poet puts it, swimming among 'the sea-beasts and archetypal monsters . . . the Easter-fish'; and as the sun of righteousness arises over the land, 'shedding his true, saving, healthful and fruitful light', it penetrates even 'into the depths of the intractable sea, transfiguring the sea-monsters into servants for himself'.[17] It was an adage of the early Christian thinkers that what had not been assumed by God, could not be healed. But, as they argued, man's whole nature has been healed, therefore there is nothing in it that was not assumed. The argument holds good today; the only difference is that we have a different, and in some respects larger, understanding of that which was assumed.

And, what is more, all that was done and all that is seen in this initial moment of incarnation is of universal import. It sheds its healing light back into the past. As Andrewes says in another sermon, quoting Pope Leo,

'the joy of it went back up to the ages past, even to Abraham's time, two thousand years and more before ever it came'.[18]

It is to be at work throughout the centuries of the future. All men are touched by it. All men are called to be reborn, to find themselves and so to grow as sons of a divine and heavenly Father. The Virgin's womb is not the only place of birth. There are also the waters of the font, which also bring forth new life. Nor is it only the first disciples who have seen with their eyes and handled with their hands. To us also the Word of life has made himself perceptible by the senses, given himself in his Body and his Blood, in a mystery, the hidden reality of the Eucharist. The sacraments, too, Andrewes tells us, are involved in the mystery of the incarnation, in the meaning of the name Emmanuel, which says that God is with us.

'With us' – to make us that to God, that he was this day to

man. And this indeed was the chief end of his being 'with us'; to give us a *posse fieri*, a capacity, 'a power to be made the sons of God', by being born again of water and of the Spirit'; for *Originem quam sumpsit ex utero Virginis posuit in fonte Baptismatis*, 'the same original that himself took in the womb of the Virgin to usward, the same hath he placed for us in the fountain of Baptism to Godward'. Well therefore called the womb of the Church *sustoichon* to the Virgin's womb, with a power given it of *concipiet et pariet filios* to God. So his being conceived and born the Son of man doth conceive and bring forth (*filiato, filiationem*), our being born, our being the sons of God. His participation of our human, our participation of His Divine nature.[19]

The marvellous interchange which the incarnation brings about could not be more clearly expressed; his descent into our human life that we might be raised into the divine life. Nor could the significance of the great initial act of baptism be more strongly indicated, with the quotation from Pope Leo, which reminds us that the Church also is mother, with a maternity which stems from the motherhood of Mary. This is not an isolated passage in Andrewes's teaching. The same doctrine recurs at Easter and Whitsun as well. God became man, in order that man might become god. He does not tire of driving home the message. This is the full scope of his faith. So in the third sermon for Whitsun he writes: 'The Holy Ghost is the Alpha and Omega of all our solemnities. In his coming down, all the feasts begin at his annunciation when he descended on the Blessed Virgin, whereby the Son of God did take our nature, the nature of man. And in the Holy Ghost's coming they end, even in his descending this day upon the sons of men, whereby they become "partakers" of his nature, the nature of God.'[20] From the annunciation to Mary to the growth of the Church all is one action of the grace of God. The theme of deification, our being made god by grace, takes its true place at the heart of the Christian teaching.

So from the sacrament of our new birth, Baptism, Andrewes goes forward, and as in all his Christmas sermons, draws his teaching to a close by applying it to the Eucharist which is about to be celebrated. Nothing demonstrates more vividly the way in which, in Andrewes's thought, theology is meant to end in worship, than these conclusions to his sermons; in them the liturgical purpose of all is revealed. What is said leads on to what is done. And here on this day, the day when the Word was made flesh, it is naturally of Christ's presence with us in the body that he wishes to speak. Christ is present with us in many ways, he says; but this day

> hath a special *cum* of itself, peculiar to it. Namely that we be so with him, as he this day was 'with us'; that was in the flesh, not in spirit only. That flesh that was conceived and this day born (*Corpus aptasti Mihi,*) that body that was this day fitted to him. And if we be not with Him thus, if this His flesh be not "with us", if we partake it not, which way soever else we be with Him, we come short of the *Im* of this day. *Im* otherwise it may be, but not that way which is proper to this feast. 'Thy land, O Immanuel', saith the Prophet in the next chapter; and may not I say, This Thy feast, Immanuel? Sure no being with Him so kindly, so pleasing to Him, so fitting this feast, as to grow into one with Him; as upon the same day, so the very same way He did 'with us'.
>
> This, as it is most proper, so it is the most straight and near that can be – the surest being withall that can be. *Nihil tam nobiscus, tam nostrum, quam alimentum nostrum*, 'nothing so with us, so sure, as that we eat and drink down', which goeth, and groweth one with us. For *alimentum et alitum* do *coalescere in unum*, 'grow into an union'; and that union is inseparable ever after. This then I commend to you, even the being with Him in the Sacrament of His Body – that Body that was conceived and born, as for other ends so for this specially, to be 'with you'; and this day, as for other intents, so even for this, for the Holy Eucharist. This as the kindliest for the time, as the surest for the manner of being with.[21]

It is interesting that one of the things which Andrewes seems concerned to emphasize here is the gradual growth into union with God, symbolized and effected by eating and drinking, two of the most basic human activities by which we assimilate things not into our minds, but into our bodies, that they may be the basis for our life. Here again, he draws out strongly the relation of the incarnation to the sacraments, though we must note that he does not do so in an exclusive way. It is not only for this end, not only for this intent that Christ has taken a body, for as he asserts at the beginning, there are many ways in which he is with us. The Eucharist must not be set alone, in splendid isolation; it is the centre of a whole network of means of grace, the heart of the mystery of the Church, and it is rightly understood when it is seen in this large and inclusive context. This whole passage of Andrewes might be an exposition of the position succinctly outlined by Hooker in the words which we have already quoted, where he asks us to consider 'how God is in Christ, then how Christ is in us, and how the Sacraments do serve to make us partakers of Christ'. Hooker and Andrewes, almost exact contemporaries, employ very different styles and methods of teaching. The development of their thought, so far as we know, went on independently of each other. It was to be of momentous importance for the whole future of Anglicanism, that in their essential conclusions they should have come so close together.

Before we leave Andrewes, we must look at part of another of these eucharistic endings, perhaps the finest and most beautiful of them all. It comes at the end of the Sixteenth Sermon on the Nativity, one which has for its text the words from Ephesians: 'That in the dispensation of the fullness of times, he might gather together into one all things, both which are in Heaven, and which are in earth, even in him.' Here Andrewes expounds the incarnation as being the fulfilment and gathering together of time, all times. Clearly he is aware of the dimension of historical time, the age-old expectation of the people of Israel, from the faith of Abraham to the faith of the Blessed Virgin. On this subject of the hope of Israel he speaks in many places, and sometimes with special reference to Abraham who rejoices 'that his seed should be his Saviour, and out his roots should rise his Redeemer; all this joy should grow from the fruit of his own body',[22] in this way making a parallel with Mary whose faith and obedience likewise knows the joy and amazement of the divine which grows in her own body. But here it is the time of the natural order, the seasons, which particularly

31

concerns him. They too have their contribution to make to the 'body' which has been prepared for the Christ.

In this theme of the recapitulation of the seasons of the year, there is an intimation of a strand of thought latent in the biblical tradition, which needs particularly to be developed and pondered at the present day. There can be no question in the Bible but that God's acts in history are specific, centring on the call and preparation of one people. But God's acts and God's concerns are also universal. The God of Abraham, Isaac and Jacob, is also the God of all men, who makes his sun to rise on just and unjust alike. This is not only a perception of the New Testament. It is there already in the Old, in the covenant made with all mankind after the disaster of the flood: 'While earth remaineth, seed-time and harvest, and cold and heat, and summer and winter, and day and night shall not cease' (Gen. 8:22). It is this covenant with all mankind to which Barnabas and Paul appeal at Lystra when they are taken to be gods, and try to turn their hearers' minds to the living God 'which made heaven and earth, the sea and all things that are therein. . . He left not himself without witness, and in that he did good and gave us food from heaven, and fruitful seasons, filling our hearts with good and gladness' (Acts 14:15–17). This doctrine of creation is by no means the whole of the gospel of God, but it is part of it without which the rest may become unearthed, unrelated to the whole of man's experience, discarnate, a mere abstract theory.

All this Mary reminds us of. She is the one, who by her very existence tells us that the Word has become flesh, has entered into all the common processes of birth and growth. In the hymns of the Eastern Church she is specifically called 'the good earth', the one 'in whom all creation rejoices'. Andrewes does not develop this thought explicitly. It comes out more clearly in some of his successors. But it is a thought which may readily occur to us, as we examine this magnificent text, with its celebration of the coming together of heaven and earth, of time and eternity, in a moment which is made real for us in 'the highest perfection we can in this life aspire unto'.

For there we do not gather to Christ or of Christ, but we gather Christ Himself; and gathering Him we shall gather the tree and fruit and all upon it. For as there is a recapitulation of all in Heaven and earth in Christ, so there is a recapitulation of all in Christ in the holy Sacrament. You may see it clearly: there is in Christ the Word eternal for things in Heaven; there is also flesh for things on earth. Semblably, the Sacrament consisteth of a Heavenly and of a terrene part, (it is Irenaeus' own words); the Heavenly – there the word too, the abstract of the other; the earthly – the element.

And in the elements, you may observe there is a fullness of the seasons of the natural year; of the corn-flour or harvest in the one, bread; of the wine-press or vintage in the other, wine. And in the heavenly, of the 'wheat-corn' whereto he compareth himself – bread, even 'the living Bread' (or 'Bread of life') 'that came down from Heaven'; the true Manna, whereof we may gather each his gomer. And again of him, the true Vine, as he calls himself – the blood of the grapes of that Vine. Both these issuing out of this day's recapitulation, both in *corpus autem aptasti mihi* of this day.'

It is as if the seasons had joined together in a universal dance, had formed themselves into a circlet or a crown for the celebration of this day.[23]

This makes in the Eucharist 'as I may say a kind of hypostatical union of the sign and the thing signified', and Andrewes cites Theodoret and Gelasius who both refer to the Eucharist to illustrate the faith that, in Christ, both humanity and divinity remain whole even though united in one. Then he takes the matter back again to argue against Rome, that in the fullness of the sacrament both are truly present, the thing signified and the sign 'still full and whole in his own kind'. And here in the Eucharist there are indeed many gatherings into one, many benefits. 'One shall serve as the sum of all; that the very end of the sacrament is to gather again to God and his favour, if it happen, as oft it doth, we scatter and stray from him. And to gather us as close and near as *alimentum alito*, that is as near as may be. And as to gather us to God, so likewise each to other mutually; expressed lively in the symbols of many grains into one, and many grapes into the other. The Apostle is plain that we are all "one bread and one body, so many as are partakers of the one bread", so moulding us as it were into one loaf together. The gathering to God refers still to things in heaven, this other to men, to the things in earth here. All under one head by the common faith; all into one body mystical by mutual charity.'[24]

NOTES

1 Richard Hooker, *The Laws of Ecclesiastical Polity*, v. l. 3
2 L. S. Thornton, *Richard Hooker*, p. 119
3 Richard Hooker, *LEP* v. lvi. 9
4 Francis Paget, in Charles Gore (ed.), *Lux Mundi*, pp. 428–9
5 Lancelot Andrewes, *Ninety-Six Sermons*. Library of Anglo-Catholic Theology, vol. 1, p. 6
6 Ibid., p. 5
7 Ibid., pp. 53–4
8 Ibid., p. 156
9 Ibid., pp. 185–6
10 Ibid., p. 192
11 Ibid., pp. 193–4
12 Henry Vaughan, *Poetry and Selected Prose*, ed. L. C. Martin (Oxford 1963), p. 342
13 Ibid., p. 139
14 Ibid., pp. 139–40
15 Ibid., p. 140
16 Ibid., p. 141
17 From the poem of D. Gwenallt Jones (1899–1968), 'Gwlad ac Ynys'. ('Country and Island'), published originally in his collection *Gwreiddiau* (Llandysul 1959) and translated and quoted by H. A. Hodges in his article on the poet in *Sobornost* Series 6, no. 1, Summer 1970, pp. 25–33
18 Op. cit., p. 122
19 Ibid., pp. 150–151
20 *Ninety-Six Sermons*, LACT, vol. iii (Oxford 1841), pp. 145–5
21 Vol. i. pp. 151–2
22 Ibid., p. 130
23 Ibid., p. 281
24 Ibid., p. 282

2

'A Collision of Joys': Jeremy Taylor

There has not been in our century any widespread interest in the writings of Lancelot Andrewes, and his works are not on the whole easy to obtain. Nevertheless, Eliot's enthusiasm for him, his quotations from him in *Gerontion* and *Ash Wednesday*, and above all in *The Coming of the Magi* have at least brought him before the notice of the reading public. The same is not true of Jeremy Taylor, whose work is if anything even more inaccessible than that of Andrewes. This fact is the more interesting in that the early nineteenth-century critics regarded Taylor as among the greatest of English writers, to be compared with Shakespeare, Milton and Bacon. Coleridge, Hazlitt, Charles Lamb all unite in his praises. This interest of the romantics in the English seventeenth century, and especially the concern of Coleridge for seventeenth-century theology is a subject which deserves further study. Coleridge found in the writers of this period, not only an exposition of the Trinitarian doctrine, in which his mind was able to rest, but also a vision of the co-inherence of man and nature which was of the utmost importance for his own understanding of man's relation to the universe. In Taylor he found a writer whose style, for all its elaboration and amplitude, is not unrelated to the content of what he is saying, and whose extended metaphors fit into a picture of the world, in which every detail is related to the whole, and the whole is present in every detail. In this connection it must be said that the selection of passages made from Taylor by Logan Pearsall Smith, half a century ago, does something of a disservice to the writer. Pearsall Smith himself believed that Taylor's beauties as a prose writer were independent of the conscious content of his writing, indeed that 'in his best writing . . . what he really says, rather than what he thinks he is saying – his unconscious rather than his conscious utterance – is the thing which is of real interest and importance to us'. He consequently drew together a collection of beautiful passages, 'imaginative prose, full of colour and music', which very soon sate us with their richness and luxuriance. While Taylor may not have been a thinker of great originality, the style of his writing is not unrelated to the nature of what he is saying.

It is true that by comparison with the closely textured prose of Andrewes, with its taut, sharp rhythms and its frequent citations of Scripture and the Fathers, we are conscious in approaching Taylor of entering a different world. The pace is leisurely; the sentences, far from being brief and packed, expand and overflow. The abundance of imagery strikes us rather than the sequence of thought. This imaginative exuberance, which has been remarked on by all commentators, did not escape the notice of his contemporaries. In the sermon preached at his funeral, George Rust, his successor in the see of Dromore, remarked in a notable sentence, 'That which did most of all captivate and enravish was the gaiety and richness of his fancy; for he had much in him of that natural enthusiasm that inspires all great poets and orators; and there was a generous ferment in his blood and spirits, that set his fancy bravely a-work, and made it swell and teem, and become pregnant to such degree of luxuriancy, as nothing but the greatness of his wit and judgement could have kept it within due bounds and measures.'[1]

The truth of this will become clear as we examine the way in which he speaks of the role of the Blessed Virgin in the scheme of redemption. If occasionally the elaboration of the style seems artificial, nonetheless we can often see a peculiar fitness in the choice of imagery to the subject being treated. Beneath the decoration a solid structure is to be discerned, and for all the difference of style it will become clear that the faith which is expressed is the same as that of Andrewes. There is, as we shall discover, a remarkable consistency of outlook in the members of this school.

The passages in which Taylor discusses our subject occur for the most part in the opening chapters of his Life of Christ, *The Great Exemplar*: an amply meditative retelling of parts of the gospel narrative. Here, reflection on the figure of Mary is by no means avoided. And Taylor finds much that we are to learn from her. She is, for him, first and foremost, the type of prayer and silent contemplation. As we shall see, he makes an elaborate contrast between her calling and that of St Paul. This may have been intended as a rebuke to any tendency to elevate her altogether above all other saints and to ascribe to her all virtues, by showing that she had those virtues proper to her estate. But it also enables him to develop his appreciation of the contemplative element in her life, in a way fully in harmony with the older tradition, common to East and West alike, which pictures her as specially dedicated to prayer. While he speaks in exuberant terms of the exaltation of her soul at the message of the angel, he also insists on the deep inner stillness which possessed her, in such a way as to suggest a profound understanding of the difference between the secret work of grace in the depths of the heart, and some of the more spectacular effects which at times accompany it. In speaking of the way in which joy necessarily communicates itself, he also stresses that the work of grace must at times be hidden, and is constantly progressing in ways and at times 'where no eye observes'. In all these passages there is a profound sense that grace fulfils nature, and that in Mary the good earth brings forth the fruit for which God originally made it.

When we come to examine these texts more closely we cannot do better than to begin with the paragraph where Taylor speaks of Mary's reaction at the time of the annunciation.

When the blessed Virgin was so ascertained, that she should be a mother and a maid, and that two glories, like the two luminaries of heaven, should meet in her, that she might in such a way become the mother of her Lord, that she might with better advantages be his servant; then all her hopes and her desires received such satisfaction, and filled all the corners of her heart so much, as indeed it was fain to make room for its reception. But she to whom the greatest things of religion, and the transportations of devotion, were made familiar, by the assiduity and piety of her daily practices, however she was full of joy, yet she was carried like a full vessel, without the violent tossings of a tempestuous passion, or the wrecks of a stormy imagination: and as the power of the Holy Ghost did descend upon her like rain into a fleece of wool, without any obstreperous noises or violences to nature, but only the extraordinariness of an exaltation, so her spirit received it with the gentleness and tranquillity fitted for the entertainment of the spirit of love, and a quietness symbolical to the holy guest of her spotless womb, the Lamb of God. . .[2]

We start here with the familiar theme of the conjunction of opposites, motherhood and virginity, and with the thought of the fulfilment of hopes and aspirations. But we pass almost immediately to the striking image of the ship in full cargo, carried forward by the strength of the gale, but not thrown about like a ship without ballast. It is an image which demands consideration. There is a recognition here of the many levels of human response to the divine activity, which while it may touch the surface and cause apparent disturbance, yet is most truly known in the depths of the human spirit, in certain hidden and basic orientations of will and desire which express themselves in the constancy of daily practice. There is a joy which is strong, which impels us forward like a great gale of wind, but which is yet silent and secure and does not disperse or agitate the human spirit. Here is a theme which Taylor underlines, the depth, the constancy of her prayer, that continual turning towards the mystery of God in faith and expectation. 'There are some curiosities so bold and determinate, as to tell the very matter of her prayer', at the moment of the annunciation 'and that she was praying for the salvation of all the world, and the revelation of the Messias. . . We have no security of the particular; but there is no piety so diffident as to require a sign to create belief that her employment at the instant was holy and religious. . .'[3] It is a typically Anglican statement, refraining from too confident a speculation, yet not refusing the substance behind the over-creative imagination of earlier writers.

This conviction about the hidden, silent centre of Mary's life finds full expression in the passage where Taylor makes his comparison between the Blessed Virgin and St Paul.

And it is not altogether inconsiderable to observe, that the holy Virgin came to a great perfection and state of piety by a few, and those modest and even external actions. St Paul travelled over the world, preached to the Gentiles, disputed against the Jews, confounded heretics, writ excellently learned letters, suffered dangers, injuries, affronts and persecutions to the height of wonder, and by these violences of life, action and patience, obtained the crown of an excellent religion and devotion. But the holy Virgin, although she engaged sometimes in an active life, and in the exercises of an ordinary and small economy and government, or ministries of a family, yet she arrived to her perfections by the means of a quiet and silent piety, the internal actions of love, devotion, and contemplation; and instructs us, that not only those who have opportunity and powers of a magnificent religion, or a pompous charity, or miraculous conversion of souls, or assiduous and effectual preachings, or exterior demonstrations of corporal mercy, shall have the greatest crown, and the addition of degrees and accidental rewards; but the silent reflections, the splendours of an internal devotion, the unions of love, humility and obedience, the daily offices of prayer and praises sung to God, the acts of faith and fear, of patience and meekness, of hope and reverence, repentance and charity, and those graces which walk in a veil and silence, make great ascents to God, and as sure progress to favours and a crown, as the more ostentatious and laborious exercises of a more solemn religion. No man needs to complain of a want of power or opportunities for religious perfections; a devout woman in her closet, praying with much zeal and affection for the conversion of souls, is in the same order to a 'shining like stars in glory' as he who by excellent discourses puts it into a more forward disposition to be actually performed. And possibly her prayers obtained energy and force to my sermon, and made the ground fruitful, and the seed spring up to life eternal.[4]

The passage is, on many levels, not unworthy of its author. Even by Taylor's standards the third sentence of the paragraph must be allowed to be ample. But behind the luxuriance of the rhetoric there is personal experience at work. At the end we suddenly become aware of the extent to which the whole comparison has been moulded by Taylor's own experience of his relationship with the devout ladies, particularly Lady Anne Carbery, who helped him during the period of the Commonwealth. We may wonder too how much this reflection on the reality and meaning of an inner life, withdrawn from external and spectacular activity, was stimulated by his own enforced retirement throughout the period of the Puritan ascendancy. The experience of persecution can have the effect of deepening and strengthening convictions which had formerly been theoretical. This seems to have been the case with Taylor. Towards the end of the 1650s, when he was living in Northern Ireland, he could write of the 'experimental and secret way' of religious progress. 'My retirement in this solitary place hath been, I hope, of some advantage to me as to this state of religion, in which I am yet but a novice. . . I beg of you to assist me with your prayers, and to obtain of God for me that I may arrive to that height of love and union with God, which is given to all those souls who are very dear to God.'[5] But behind and through these personal considerations, we can surely see something more; a profound conviction about the meaning of a life wholly given to the inner work of prayer; some intuition, some glimpse of the meaning of the contemplative life, still vividly present in the seventeenth century, despite the absence of monastic communities. It gives us an insight into the quality of seventeenth-century religion and the depth of prayer which lies behind Taylor's liturgical interests and projects. Man's life can expand and unfold, can grow and mature towards God inwardly as well as outwardly. There is an inner journey, as well as an outer one, with its own dangers and temptations. 'Those graces which walk in a veil and silence' – the phrase is one which justifies Taylor's older reputation as a stylist – 'make great ascents to God'.

But this is not the only phrase of an exceptional beauty to be found in this section of Taylor's work. Another occurs in the passage where he is meditating on the fact that Mary had apparently not told Joseph of the message of the angel. 'It is in some circumstances and from some persons more secure to conceal visions and those heavenly gifts, which create estimates among men, than to publish them, which may possibly minister to vanity; and those exterior graces may do God's work, though no observer note them, but the person for whose sake they are sent: like rain falling in uninhabited valleys, where no eye observes the showers; yet the valleys laugh and sing to God in their refreshment without a witness.'[6] How powerfully the picture of rain falling in lonely upland valleys where no eye observes it, suggests the continued, silent generosity of the divine activity, always at work throughout the whole creation, effective in ways we neither know nor understand, causing the earth to laugh and sing to God its creator. The image itself puts before us the idea of the Blessed Virgin as the type of the receptivity and fruitfulness of the order of nature, springing up in response to the initiative of God. It is an idea which constantly recurs when men begin to meditate on her calling.

However, it is not only the secret work of God which Taylor celebrates in his meditation on the life of the Virgin as it is portrayed by St Luke. There is also the visitation to consider. 'And she, who was now full of God, bearing God in her virgin womb, and the Holy Spirit in her heart, who had also overshadowed her, enabling her to a supernatural and miraculous conception, arose with haste and gladness to communicate that joy which was designed for the world. . . And Mary arose in those days and went into the hill country with haste, into a city of Judah.'[7] If there are circumstances which indicate that we should hide the gifts which are given us, and conceal our joys, nevertheless of itself joy is something to be shared, something which communicates itself to all with whom we enter into contact. Taylor does not hesitate to use all the resources of his eloquence at its most flamboyant in his attempt to communicate the exaltation and amazement of this meeting of Mary with Elizabeth.

But the joys that the Virgin Mother had, were such as concerned all the world; and that part of them which was her peculiar, she would not conceal from persons apt to their entertainment, but go publish God's mercy towards her to another holy person, that they might join in the praises of God; as knowing that though it may be convenient to represent our personal necessities in private, yet God's gracious returns and the blessings he makes to descend on us, are more fit, when there

41

is no personal danger collaterally appendant, to be published in the communion of saints; that the hopes of others may receive increase, that their faith may grow up to become excellent and great, and the praises of God may be sung aloud, till the sound strike at heaven, and join with the hallelujahs, which the morning stars in their orbs pay to their great Creator.[8]

The rejoicing of man, when it is redoubled in being shared, acquires a dimension of cosmic celebration.

It is not easy to imagine what a collision of joys was at this blessed meeting: two mothers of two great princes, the one the greatest that was born of woman, and the other was his Lord, and these made mothers by two miracles, met together with joy and mysteriousness; where the mother of our Lord went to visit the mother of his servant, and the Holy Ghost made the meeting a festival, and descended upon Elizabeth, and she prophesied. Never but in heaven was there more joy and ecstasy. The persons . . . meeting together to compare and unite their joys and their eucharist, and then made prophetical and inspired, must needs have discoursed like seraphim and the most ecstasied order of intelligences; for all the faculties of nature were turned into grace, and expressed in their way the excellent solemnity. 'For it came to pass when Elizbaeth heard the salutation of Mary, the babe leaped in her womb; and Elizabeth was filled with the Holy Ghost.'[9]

This comparison with the orders of angels is one which we have already met in Andrewes. Here it is expressed with the extravagance of a baroque rhetoric, but for all that it is no less serious. It has its basis in those passages in the Bible which speak of man being created but little lower than the angels, in order to be crowned with glory and honour, and again in the words of St Paul when he declared that Christ took on him the seed of Abraham, and not the nature of angels. These are all passages which are intended to express the heights to which human nature is called, the true capacity of man, as revealed in the mystery of the incarnation. The faith which they embody was carried on into the tradition of the Church, and became a staple element in the hymns of the liturgy.

Even if we find it difficult to accept all the traditional picture of the angelic realm, the comparison need not be without meaning for us. Principalities and powers, of one kind or another, are very familiar to us. Impersonal forces, for good or evil, which seem infinitely stronger and more permanent than man in his frailty and transience, these we know well. The message of the gospel is that over all these man's personal life is triumphant, for God is within man, has united man with himself, has proved victorious over every power. The meeting of two pregnant women in an obscure Palestinian village is of greater significance than all these forces. Man's life, even in its most ordinary and routine aspects has a hidden wealth of possibilities which is infinite with God's infinity.

But it is not only this point which is so striking in the two passages which have been quoted here. What cannot escape the reader is the consistently liturgical character of the thought and terminology. The liturgy is not only a meeting of man with God, it is also a meeting of man with man, a *synaxis*, a coming together into one place. Joy and thanksgiving are things to be shared, which grow by being shared, and when this happens something which involves the whole universe begins to take place. The united praise and thanksgiving of men, their common prayer, rises up in unity with the praises of all creation. In this sense the meeting of Mary and Elizabeth is a beginning of Christian liturgy, and the words which the Evangelist has given to them in this moment have remained a constant part of the Church's worship. Taylor was not at all unaware of the Eastern Church's teaching about the role of the Holy Spirit in the Church's sacraments; like many of the Anglicans of his period he was much influenced by his study of the Eastern liturgies. So he can write of the original moment, 'the Holy Ghost made the meeting festival'. In the power of the Holy Spirit, man's coming together to praise God is transformed into a coming together of man with God in the festival of the Kingdom; the Eucharist of man is lifted up into the life and energy of God. So, too, Taylor can speak at this point of the 'excellent solemnity', a term which suggests the formula of the Latin rite, which frequently speaks of the Church's festivals as 'joyful solenities', as if to join together reminiscences of both Eastern and Western liturgical tradition.[10]

In the very phrase the 'excellent' or 'joyful solemnity', we have a junction of apparent opposites which is strange to our society, but which was more natural in a society in which festival was, though contested, still widely understood. Perhaps it was because the Church's traditional festivals, with their mixture of Christian and pre-Christian, religious and social, human and divine were so much threatened at this time, that the Anglicans had so sharp a sense of the richness of their meaning. To Taylor it is clear that a solemnity is something weighty, serious, ordered and ceremonious. It is also something ecstatic, jubilant, joyful and liberating. These things are only apparent contradictions. In fact they are complementary. Man's life, both personal and social, cannot become truly human unless it contains both elements, unless it is able to unite joy and sorrow, gravity and lightness in a single complex unity of love. Throughout this passage there is an evident awareness of festival and solemnity, and an experience of a joy which is truth telling and truth revealing; of the mingling of human and divine which is one of the characteristic notes of Christian worship, and which derives from the union of man with God in Christ, which is the heart of its message of goodness. 'For all the faculties of nature were turned into grace, and expressed in their way the excellent solemnity.' The many different faculties of man, feeling, willing, thinking, acting are brought together into one, integrated and made whole when the Holy Spirit touches the human spirit in the act of worship. All man's being from the root up, from the very 'groundsill' as Andrewes says, is liberated into the kingdom of God's grace.

Taylor, of course, thinks of this meeting of Mary and Elizabeth as unique. He speaks of 'two mothers of two great princes'. But he knows that these princes are so only in a hidden, paradoxical way. And though indeed on any Christian reckoning this meeting was unique, yet it is implied that it was also universal. The meeting of any two people when the Holy Spirit makes 'the meeting festival', may be filled with 'joy and mysteriousness'. The meeting of two women carrying in their bodies, as well as in their hope and love, the promises of two new, unknown lives may be doubly so. We learn something here not only about the nature of liturgical celebration, but also of personal relationship. Again the hidden potential of humanity is revealed.

Both thoughts are present in the words with which Taylor introduces his meditation on the Magnificat.

The blessed Virgin Mary hearing her cousin full of spirit and prophecy, calling her blessed, and praising her faith, and confirming her joy, instantly sang her hymn to God, returning those praises, which she received, to him to whom they did appertain. For so we should worship God with all our praises, being willing upon no other condition to extend our hand to receive our own honour, but that with the other we might transmit it to God; that as God is honoured in all his creatures, so he may be honoured in us too; looking upon the graces which God hath given us, but as greater instruments and abilities to serve him, being none of ours, but talents which are intrusted into our banks to be improved.[11]

The thought is a profound one. The circulation of divine life, which comes out from God into the creation, returns to God enriched with the gratitude of man, having received a human form. In hidden, unknown ways, no less than in the public thanksgiving, the Eucharist of the Christian assembly, God's glory is made known and the creation itself is glorified in him.

In his meditation on the theme of Mary as mother, it appears more than once that Taylor is anxious to avoid any tendency to disparage marriage in comparison with virginity. Both estates are good, both to be honoured. He himself was married twice, and in his writings as a whole we can find a certain fluctuation of view, at times an exaltation of virginity, as for instance in *Holy Living*, where in some sections he envisages the situation of 'virgins that offer that state to God, and mean not to enter into the state of marriage', and at times an exaltation of married life. Here he attempts to keep a balance.

When the eternal God meant to stoop so low as to be fixed to our centre, he chose for his mother a holy person and a maid, yet affianced to a just man, that he might not only be secured in the innocency, but also provided for in the reputation of his mother . . .

And yet her marriage was more mysterious; for as, besides the miracle it was an eternal honour and advancement to the glory of virginity, that he chose a virgin for his mother, so it was in that manner attempered, that the Virgin was betrothed, lest honourable marriage might be disrupted, and seem inglorious, by a positive rejection from any participation of the honour. . .[12]

It is this concern for the honour of marriage and for the meaning of maternity, which seems to lie behind the *First Discourse*, or excursus, which punctuates *The Great Exemplar*, and which has as its subject, 'Of nursing children'. An earlier generation than our own, which had not known the work of Freud and Klein, might have been surprised at the amount of space which Taylor gives to this discussion of the importance of breastfeeding, and of the value of the mother herself nursing her child. Taylor still lives in a world which can take the psychosomatic unity of men as a given and commonly understood reality. We live in a time which is seeking to recover this insight. For him it is clear that man's higher, more spiritual acts and virtues are all rooted in his most basic bodily needs and instincts. The virtues, the distinctively human qualities and actions all grow from this physical basis which man shares with the animals. The question of feeding infants may seem at first sight a trivial one, but in so far as it is through its relationship with its mother that the child's capacity for relationship with other people and with the outside world is first exercised and developed, it is not trivial at all.

> Although other actions are more perfect and spiritual, yet this is more natural and humane; other things being superadded to a full duty, rise higher, but this builds stronger, and is like a part of the foundation, having no lustre, but much strength; and however the others are full of ornament, yet this hath in it some degree of necessity, and possibly is with more danger and irregularity omitted, than actions, which spread their leaves fairer, and look more gloriously.[13]

If the foundations are not well laid the whole subsequent work of building will suffer.

It is not surprising that there is no other section of the Life of Christ in which Taylor reflects at such length on the place of Mary, as in these opening chapters. But he cannot omit to speak of her when he comes to meditate on the crucifixion. Nor does his eloquence desert him here. But what is more striking is the degree in which he is faithful to his first conviction about her. Just as the joys of the annunciation were not enough to overthrow her inner silence of spirit, so even the grief of the crucifixion, the sword which goes through her own heart, meets in her heart a greater reality of calm and steadfast love.

By the cross of Christ stood the holy Virgin-mother, upon whom old Simeon's prophecy was now verified; for now she felt 'a sword piercing through her very soul'; she stood without clamour and womanish noises; sad, silent, and with a modest grief, deep as the waters of the abyss, but smooth as the face of a pool; full of love, and patience, and sorrow and hope. Now she was put to it to make use of all those excellent discourses her holy Son had used to build up her spirit, and fortify it against this day. Now she felt the blessings and strengths of faith; and she passed from the griefs of the passion to the expectation of the resurrection; and she rested in this death, as in a sad remedy; for she knew it reconciled God with all the world. But her hope drew a veil before her sorrow; and though her grief was great enough to swallow her up, yet her love was greater, and did swallow up her grief.[14]

Such lines can, of course, give us no historical information about the attitude of the Blessed Virgin at this moment. The modern exegete will rightly remind us that the gospel tells us directly nothing whatsoever about it, though the narrative in the Fourth Gospel is eloquent enough, for all its economy. But as we read them, we may well think of countless representations of the crucifixion in which the mother of the crucified man is depicted as calm and upright, in contrast with the distraught grief of the other onlookers. These are things which represent profound convictions about the nature of grief; that the truest and strongest thoughts and feelings are often ones which lie too deep for outward expression whether in word or gesture; that a great calm need not be a sign either of indifference or insensibility; but that in those whose lives have been hidden in God in constant prayer, such calm may be a reflection of an inner stability based in the constant love of God himself, 'deep as the waters of the abyss, but smooth as the face of a pool'. We are reminded of Taylor's earlier words about the serenity of the mother in the moment of her greatest joy. Here is a similar intuition, which may well lead us to a reticence like that of the gospel narratives.

NOTES

1 *The Whole Works of the Rt. Revd. Jeremy Taylor* (1835), vol. i, p. lxx
2 Ibid., p. 28
3 Ibid., p. 29
4 Ibid., pp. 29–30
5 Quoted in Margaret Cropper, *Flame Touches Flame* (1949), p. 143
6 Op. cit., p. 32
7 Ibid., p. 30
8 Ibid., p. 31
9 Ibid., p. 31
10 For an excellent study of Taylor's work as a liturgist see H. Boone Porter, *Jeremy Taylor, Liturgist* (1978). Dr Porter stresses the way in which Taylor brings together Eastern and Western influences in his liturgical work.
11 Op. cit., p. 32
12 Ibid., p. 29
13 Ibid., p. 38
14 Ibid., p. 340

3

'The Virgin Mother, the Eternal Son': Mark Frank

If neither Andrewes nor Taylor is widely read at present, their names at least are fairly familiar. This is not the case with Mark Frank, who on any ordinary reckoning would have to be judged one of the secondary figures of this period. Dying in 1664, at the age of fifty-one, Frank did not have time to reach the eminence which would surely have been his, had he lived longer. Fellow of Pembroke College, Cambridge, and after the restoration of the monarchy Master of the College, Frank reveals himself in his sermons a true disciple in the school of Lancelot Andrewes. In his preaching the balanced theology of this period of Anglican divinity, nourished on Scripture and the Fathers alike, finds eloquent expression. Indeed of all the Anglican preachers of this time he speaks most fully about Mary; and we are not surprised to find in him a powerful sense of the meaning of the liturgy, and of the place of man's body in his approach to God. It is some measure of the richness of the seventeenth century that we can find writing of such quality in one who is so little known.

There is in Frank's sermons, at times, a sharp polemical note, occasioned by the controversies with the Puritans. When we reflect that some of the sermons which we have, must have been preached during the Commonwealth, in private, semi-clandestine assemblies, at a time when Frank was deprived of his fellowship, this is hardly surprising. What is more striking is the generally serene way in which he expounds his teaching and seeks to find a *via media* between the clashing opinions of his contemporaries. We can hear in him an outstanding spokesman of that older way of seeing things, which was soon to collapse under the impact of the philosophy of Descartes and the first beginnings of scientific inquiry. He still thinks with confidence of a man as a microcosm placed at the centre of a universe where all is inter-related. He can still employ that highly metaphysical style which sees a detailed correspondence between man's inner and outer world. It is interesting to speculate whether, had he lived another twenty years, he could have continued to preach in this same style, and with the same emphasis.

Since Frank's sermons are virtually unknown, and since he is a preacher who needs to be quoted at length we shall not hesitate to make lengthy quotations from them, gradually becoming familiar with his theological method and approach, before we come to see what he has to say specifically on the subject of Mary. His exposition of the place of Mary in the scheme of redemption needs to be seen in context if it is to be evaluated properly. The theme of joy in God, and its proper expression, which we have already seen in Andrewes and in Taylor, is one which finds eloquent expression in his work. It is a subject which demands our attention in this connection. So in a sermon for Easter we read

> . . . the joy that God requires in the things that he has made, or any time makes for us, is not only inward, it must issue out into outward acts; out into the mouth to sing forth his praise, 'in psalms and hymns and spiritual songs'; out into the feet to go up to the house of God with the posture as well as the voice of joy and gladness, to go up with haste, to worship with reverence, to stand up cheerfully at the hymns and songs of praise; our very bones, as David speaks, to rejoice too; the very clattered bones to clatter together and rejoice; all the parts and powers of the body to make some expression in their way and order.'[1]

Joy, as Frank constantly teaches, is something which makes us grow, which makes for an expansion of man's heart and mind, an expansion which is to find personal and inward expression, and also to have social and ethical consequences. It is very striking in the passage below, that the social and economic dimensions of man's life are involved, no less than those which we are apt to call strictly religious. Speaking of the 'exceeding joy' which the Wise

Men knew when they found the way to Bethlehem, he says in an Epiphany sermon,

> Being so exceeding, it will exceed also the narrow compass of the inward man, will issue out also into the outward, into the tongue and head. Joy is the dilatation, the opening of the heart, and sending out the spirits into all the parts. And if this joy we have, it will open our hearts to praise him; open our hearts to heaven to receive its influence; open our hearts to our needy brother, to compassionate and relieve him; it will send out life, and heat, and spirit into all our powers – into our lips, to sing unto him, into our fingers, to play to him, into our feet, even to leap for joy; into our eyes, perpetually to gaze upon him; into our hands, to open them for his sake plentifully to the poor; into the whole body, to devote it wholly to his service. This is the wise men's joy, 'great' and 'exceeding'.[2]

Generosity to those who need, inward exaltation of spirit, outward participation in the Christian assembly, all these things go together, when God breathes his own life into the dry, scattered bones of man's existence and raises him up into true humanity, drawing together body and soul in a unity of adoration, and opening man's life alike to heaven and to his neighbour.

> But not the powers of the body alone, but all the powers of the soul too: 'Praise the Lord, O my soul, and all that is within me praise his holy name'. Our souls magnify the Lord, our spirits rejoice in God our Saviour; our memories recollect and call to mind his benefits and what he has done for us; our hearts evaporate into holy flames and ardent affections and desires after him; our wills henceforward to give up themselves wholly to him as their only hope and joy. It is no perfect joy where any of them is wanting. It is but dissembled joy where all is outward. It is but imperfect gladness where all is within. It must be both. God this day raised the body, the body therefore must raise itself, and rise up to praise him. He this day gave us hope he would not leave our souls in hell; fit, therefore, it is the soul should leave all to praise him that sits in heaven. He is not worthy of the day or the benefit of the day, worthy to be raised again, who

will not this day rise to praise; not worthy to rise at the resurrection of the just who will not rise today in the congregation of the righteous to testify his joy and gladness in the resurrection of his Saviour and his own.[3]

The fullness of joy then involves the integration of all the faculties of man. The theme which we have found in Jeremy Taylor is found again here. This joy leads man out beyond himself into the very life of God. The great insistence on the participation of the body in this life is particularly significant. We need to see it in a large historical perspective. As Aelred Squire remarks, 'Particularly in the West one of the unobserved consequences of the Schism with the East was that, with the development of the scholastic movement, a schism between flesh and spirit was gradually established both in theory and practice. Reinforced by the philosophy of Descartes, and accentuated by the social results of the Industrial Revolution, this cleavage between the bodily and the spiritual has left us in our own period with a Christianity unbelievably discarnate.'[4]

This is the version of Christianity against which many of our contemporaries have revolted, most notably those concerned with ecology and with the rediscovery of man's place in the material world. Many indeed have supposed that this 'unbelievably discarnate' form of religion is itself Christianity. No one can deny its influence in the West particularly in the Puritan movement and in those forms of Protestantism which have minimized the importance of the sacraments and distrusted the whole realm of the symbolical. But Frank stands for an older and wider tradition of classical Christian faith and understanding. This is a tradition rooted in the Bible no less than in the life of the early Christian centuries. Here it is understood that man in his totality is redeemed; that he can offer the whole of his life, body no less than soul and spirit to the service of God. This vision is central in the work of the seventeenth-century Anglicans. It lies behind their concern for the details of ceremonial in worship, a concern which has seemed to some commentators fussy and unbalanced. As Nicholas Ferrar insisted in one of his last conversations with his brother John, 'It is the right, good old way you are in; keep it. God will be worshipped in spirit and truth, in soul and in body. He will have both inward love and fear, and outward reverence of body and gesture.'⁵

This same concern lies behind their insistence on the keeping of the Church's festivals and in the celebration of the feasts of the Church, which thus become anticipations, foretastes of the feast of the Kingdom, that celebration of life and joy for which the world was made in the beginning, to which it will be drawn in the end of all things. In the feasts, and above all in the Eucharist, eternity enters into time, and time is taken up into eternity.

Again, it may be that the abolition of the festivals under the Commonwealth contributed to the particularly vivid perception which Frank has of their significance. Certainly he has a wonderful perception of the meaning of liturgical time. He gives us one of the few seventeenth-century Anglican sermons of the transfiguration, and dwells with pleasure on the origin of the name 'Candlemas', the Feast of the Presentation. The very multiplicity of the festivals is full of meaning to him. They seek, in time, to reveal something of the richness and the generosity of the divine being and the divine action. They also succeed in drawing together all the diversities of the human race. They are all occasions of blessing.

For this day also of his presentation, as well as those others of his birth, circumcision and manifestation – Candlemas-day as well as Christmas-day, New Year's day, or Epiphany, is a day of blessing; a day of God's blessing us, and our blessing of him again; of Christ's being presented for us, and our presenting to him again; of his presenting in the temple, and our presenting ourselves in the Church, to bless God and him for his presentation, his presentation-day and our Candlemas, our little candles, our petty lights, our souls reflecting back to this great light, that was this day presented in the temple and then darted down upon us.

The shepherds blessed God in the morn of his nativity; the wise men upon Epiphany; Simeon and Anna, today. All conditions before, all sexes today; ignorant shepherds and learned clerks, poor countrymen and great princes, no condition out before, and both sexes in today. Sinners both of Jew and Gentile, men that most stood in need of a Saviour, before; just and righteous souls today; that we might know there is none so good but stands in need of him one day or other – that will want a Saviour, if not at Christmas, yet at Candlemas; if not among sinners, yet among the righteous, either first or last. Mary the blessed, Joseph the just, Simeon the devout, Anna the religious, all in today, as at the end of Christmas; like the chorus to the angels' choir, to bear a part in the angels' anthem, to make up a full choir of voices to glorify God for this great present, which brings peace to the earth, and good-will among men.[6]

We cannot but be struck, in this passage, by the preacher's appreciation of the significance of this whole cycle of the feasts of Christmas, all of which are feasts of the incarnation. All of them necessarily involve our Lady and in all of them we ourselves are involved with her. Frank's use of the vernacular names for the feasts is also significant. It suggests a regard for the popular traditions surrounding them, and links with the thought that men of all conditions are to be drawn together, into the festival of faith. The Church in its worship is inclusive and catholic. There is nothing narrow or sectarian about it. This point is made again in the first of his Advent sermons, where Frank quotes St John Chrysostom on the monastic life, in order to stress that all, secular and religious alike, are called to take their part in the universal act of thanksgiving. 'Nor were these multitudes choirs of priests and clerks, or only orders of religious men; it was a congregation of seculars, though there were priests and Apostles in it. It is St Chrysostom's own note, to tell us, men are not to put off the work of devotion and religion wholly to the priest and clerk, as if they only were to sing the Benedictus, Hosannas or Alleluiahs, and the multitudes only stand looking on; or think men in some religious orders were only obliged to live orderly and like Christians, all secular or laymen as they pleased. *Non ita sane, non ita est*, says he, "It is not so indeed, it is not so." '[7] This is a passage of interest not only in that it tells us that men of all kinds are to take their share in the Church's celebration, but also because it seems to assume that the Church will include as well as laymen, priests and clerks, 'men in some religious orders', 'orders of religious men', an assumption not very common among seventeenth-century Anglicans. But all are to unite in the celebration of God's gift; and all the feasts of the year made present different aspects of this one reality. The gift of eternity is made now in the liturgy of the Church. We may suspect that when Frank speaks of glorifying God 'for this great present', there is a double meaning, either consciously or unconsciously there.

It is in the mystery of the Eucharist, that this presence is above all made known. Here the reality of the incarnation is made present with us. Like Andrews, Frank never isolates the coming of Christ in the sacrament from his other ways of coming to us, but he does not hesitate to place this mystery at the centre.

And there is a visit he is now coming today to make us, as much to be wondered at as any, – that he should feed us with his body, and yet that be in heaven; and that he should cheer us with his blood, and yet that shed so long ago; that he should set his throne and keep his table and presence upon the earth, and yet heaven his throne and earth his footstool; that he should here pose all our understandings with his mysterious work, and so many ages of Christians, after so many years of study and assistance of the Spirit, not yet be able to understand it. 'What is man, or 'the son of man', O blessed Jesu, that thou shouldst thus also visit and confound him with the wonders of thy mercy and goodness?

Here also is glory and honour too, to be admitted to his table; nowhere so great; to be made one with Him, as the meat is with the body; no glory like it. Here is the crown of plenty: fullness of pardon, grace, and heavenly benediction. Here is the crown of glory; nothing but rays and beauties, lustres and glories, to be seen in Christ, and darted from him into pious souls. Come take your crowns, come compass yourselves with those eternal circlings.

Take now the 'cup of salvation', and remember God for so remembering you: call upon the name of the Lord, and give glory to your God. If you cannot speak out fully (as who can speak, in such amazements as these thoughts may seriously work in us?) cast yourselves down in silence, and utter out your souls in these or the like broken speeches: What is man, Lord what is man? . . . What shall I say? How shall I sufficient admire?[8]

Here again we find the tone of serious ecstasy which we have discovered in Andrewes. The mind falls silent before the mystery, which so many centuries of study and reflection have not been able to fathom. In the Eucharist the fullness of God's love is made present before us, the greatness of man's calling is revealed. We recognize the coming together in one of heaven and earth, past and present, God and man; they are gathered together into a circle, a crown, an emblem of eternity. Man's life is crowned, finds its fulfilment in the eternity for which he was made in the beginning. 'Let us crown his altars then with offerings, and his name with praise; let us be often *in corona*, in the congregation of them that praise him, among such as keep holiday. Let us crown his courts with beauty, crown ourselves with good works; they should be our glory and our crown: and for the worship that he crowns us with too, let us worship and give him honour, so remember, so visit, so crown him again. . .'[9]

One of the salient facts that we know about Mark Frank's life is his close association as a young man with the family at Little Gidding. He seems to have been a particularly close friend of Nicholas Ferrar junior, the nephew of the elder Nicholas Ferrar who was the spiritual director of the whole enterprise. It was Mark Frank who composed the epitaph for the brilliant young man. It is not altogether surprising that we do not find any direct references to the family of Little Gidding in the sermons of Mark Frank. But knowing, as we do, of his connection with them, we can hardly fail to find traces of the influence of their life in his preaching. There is his evident feeling for such monastic practices as fasting and watching, his sense that the Church includes men in religious orders, his sense of the reality of prayer and the full dimensions of joy; all things which he would have seen in practice in the life of the Ferrars, and some of them things not widely appreciated among seventeenth-century Anglicans. There is a certain air of light and beauty in all the descriptions of their common life at Little Gidding which finds expression in these sermons too.

It is reported of St Lucian the Martyr, that he converted many by his modest, cheerful and pious look and carriage; and of St Bernard, that, *In carne ejus apparebat gratia quaedam spiritualis*, etc., 'There appeared a kind of spiritual grace throughout his body'; there shone a heavenly brightness in his face; there darted an angelical purity and dove-like simplicity from his eyes; so great was the inward beauty of his inward man, that it poured out itself in his whole outward man abundantly over all his parts and powers; no motion in them but reason and religion. Where such virtue is, it will be 'known', must be too: must be so expressed that men may know and feel the benefits and effects.[10]

We feel ourselves, in such a passage, to be in contact with a man who has some direct knowledge of what he is speaking about, who himself has seen men and women who have impressed him in this way. This impression becomes all the stronger in a remark which occurs in the sermon for St Stephen's Day. 'Sometimes it is (oftener it has been when the beginning of Christianity needed it at first), that by some visible comforts and discoveries he shows himself to the dying saint. Often it is that the soul ready to depart feels some sensible joys and ravishments to uphold its ailing spirits.'[11] The story of Nicholas Ferrar's deathbed, his sudden raising up of himself at the very moment when he was accustomed to rise for prayer, his exclamation, 'I have been at a feast . . . at the feast of the great King', his sudden passing – all these things must have been familiar to Mark Frank, and they can hardly have been absent from his mind when he wrote these words.

So the order and the beauty of the life which he saw at Little Gidding entered deeply into his heart and mind. On the subject of order he writes at the beginning of a sermon for St Peter's Day, 'I begin with St Peter's ill success, and that is no comfortable beginning; but it is the beginning of the text, and I love order everywhere, though it cost never so dear to keep that.'[12] We are not surprised to find an Anglican of his period emphatic on the necessity of order. But on the subject of beauty he has yet finer things to say. 'Christ's beauty is God's blessing; all beauty is so, be it what it will; from him it comes, is but a ray of that eternal beauty, that inaccessible light, that *summe pulchrum* as well as *summe bonum*, the everlasting brightness of the Father; all the beauty of the mind and body, all the integrity and vigour of all our powers, are merely from his blessing, not our merit – a good lesson from it, not to be proud of any of them.'13

This restoration of the integrity and vigour of the powers of man is a thing which has consequences for all creation; for the praise of God which rises up from all things is to become vocal and articulate through man. In the psalms of David all things are said to praise God, and in a strange passage Frank enumerates them all, one by one. Then he continues: 'Yet how should all these things we mentioned do it? Many of them have no tongue to say, many no sense to understand it. Why, they do it yet.' All things can praise God in and through man, who is the priest of nature. So in this Christmas sermon, the preacher goes on:

The sun by day, the moon by night, may become torches to light his servants' service. The earth brings forth her corn and wine to furnish out his table; the deep gives up her riches, and brings home golds and silks to adorn his holy altars; the earth brings stones and minerals, the hills and mountains trees and cedars to his house; the fire kindles tapers for it; all the meteors of the air, and all the seasons of the years, do somewhat; every wind blows somewhat towards it. The very birds and swallows get as near the altar as they can to bless him; the snow and cold and ice crowd as near Christmas as they can, to bear a part in this great solemnity, in our solemnest thanksgivings. Only he that has no need of this visit, no need of Christ or his redemption, that cares not to be saved, needs keep no Christmas, may stand out, or sit, or do what he will, at his Benedictus.

But, sure, when all things else this come in throngs to bless him, and even ice and snow come hot and eager to this feast, and willingly melt themselves into his praises, we should not, methinks, come coldly on to bless him, but come and bring our families and children and neighbours with us, to make the choir as full as possibly we can. Tell one another what Christ did today, what he every day does for us; how he visited us today, how he still visits us every morning; how he redeemed us today, how he does day by day, from one ill or other; how he began today to raise up salvation for us, and will not leave raising it for us till we can rise no higher. Tell we our children next, how in this God had respect to David his anointed, and that they must learn to have so. How he had regard to David his servant; will have so to them if they be his servants: let them therefore be sure they be so; fit them thus to sing their parts betimes in hymns, and anthems, and praises to their God; that they that cannot speak, may yet lisp it out; and when they can speak out, sing it loud and shrill, that the hollow vaults and arches may echo and rebound his praises: not your children only, but stones also be thus raised up for children unto Abraham.[14]

In this way, in man, the praises of animate and inanimate nature are joined together. All things centre themselves on him, and work together for his good, when he is fulfilling his vocation of acting towards God on behalf of all things. For man is a little world, and there is that in him which answers to all the changes and variety in the world around him. The vision so wonderfully expressed in the poetry of George Herbert, above all in the poem called simply 'Man', here finds in prose a no less eloquent exposition. In a passage where he insists on the part played by man's body as well as his soul, Frank describes this correspondence very fully.

And of the seasons there are some, you know, more acceptable than others; two very acceptable and pleasant in the year, the spring and the summer. There are the same in the souls of men; a spring, when our graces and virtues begin to sprout and blossom, bespread and clothe this earth we carry; when the Sun of Righteousness begins to smile and warm us; when the air grows temperate, our passions and affections moderate within us, and all our powers breathe nothing but violets and roses; this, as the prophet styles it, 'the very time of love'; a disposition and a time we cannot but be accepted in, wherein God begins to be in love with us. There is a summer too, when 'the hills' – the highest pitch and spirit of our souls – 'stand thick with corn', and 'the valleys' – our lowest powers, our inferior passions – 'laugh and sing'; when the bright rays of heaven shine hot upon us; when we are hung full with all heavenly fruits; when our hearts do even 'burn within us', and the whole desires even of our flesh, this dust that covers us, are on fire for heaven; when our hearts 'pant after the living brooks', and our 'souls are athirst for God', to come unto him, to 'appear before him'. This, indeed, is not only the time, but the fullness of it; when, coming so replenished with grace and righteousness, we shall be fully accepted, and be sure not to be sent empty away.[15]

It is indeed striking in this passage to see how the images of spring and summer are used to describe the development of man's life, his joy in being, and knowing himself to be, a son of God. Not only our higher faculties are fulfilled, 'our lowest powers, our inferior passions' rejoice as well. Nothing is to be left out, all has a part to play in the harmony of the whole. All is created by God, all is redeemed in Christ. As we shall see, when we come to look at Mark Frank's sermons on our Lady, this thought plays an important part in his understanding of her blessedness.

We have seen enough of the preaching of Mark Frank to be able to perceive that he stands in the tradition of Hooker and Andrewes, and rejoices to affirm the faith of the wholeness of the Christian tradition. Preaching on Christmas Day on the text from Psalm 45, 'Thou art fairer than the children of men', and applying the words to Christ, he says:

The Fathers have so expounded it before us; the Church has added authority to it by the choice of the Psalm for a part of the Office of the Day: nay, St Paul has so applied it. So I am in no ways singular; indeed I love not to be in such points as these; I tread the ancient track; though I confess I think I can never take occasions enough – not I, nor any else – to speak of Christ, of his beauty and grace and blessedness, either today or any day, though every day whatsoever.[16]

And then at once, having evoked the authority of the Fathers, he brings forward one of the fundamental qualities of all their approach to the things of God, saying 'with St Hilary, *Filium mens mea veretur attingere, et trepidat omnis sermo se prodere*, I can neither think without a kind of fear, nor speak without a kind of trembling, of a person of that glory.'[17] This appeal to the authority of the Fathers is not a mere matter of external conformity. It implies thinking with them, feeling with them, sharing their own amazement before the mystery of God in man, of man in God.

In an Easter sermon, when he is applying the verse of Psalm 118, 'This is the day which the Lord hath made . . .' to the matter of feasts, he cites Andrewes explicitly: 'And of this day of the resurrection, the Fathers, the Church, the Scriptures understand it. Not one of the Fathers, says that devout and learned Bishop Andrewes, that he had read, (and he had read many), but interpret it of Easter-day.' And Frank brings forward the evidence of the liturgy to show how the mind of the Church has shaped itself. 'The Church picks out this Psalm today, as a piece of service proper to it. This very verse in particular, was anciently used every day in Easter week; evidence enough how she understood it.'[18]

The affirmation which is implicit in such remarks of the value of unity and tradition for understanding the Christian faith and fully entering into the Christian life comes out very clearly in the Third Sermon on Whitsunday. Frank asserts that it is the Scripture which provides the primary way by which the Spirit leads us into all truth. But, he says, not the Scripture alone for

> this may all men pretend to, and everyone turns it how he lists. We must add a second. And the second is the Church, for we must know this, says St Peter; know it first too – that no Scripture is of any private interpretation. . . When men unlearned or ungrounded, presume to be interpreters, or even learned men to prefer their private senses before the received ones of the Church, it is never like to produce better. The 'pillar' and 'ground' upon which truth stands and stays is the Church, if St Paul may be allowed to be the judge.[19]

And the Church to which Frank makes appeal is no invisible or notional body. It is the Church of all the centuries.

> Indeed in itself it is most ridiculous to think the custom, and practice and order, and interpretation of all times and Churches should be false, and those of yesterday only true, unless we can think the Spirit of truth has been fifteen or sixteen hundred years asleep, and never waked till now of late; or can imagine that Christ should found a Church, and promise to be with it to the

end of the world, and then leave it presently to Antichrist to be guided by him for above fifteen hundred years together.[20]

For Frank there can be no question but that we must constantly appeal to 'the Scriptures interpreted by the perpetual practice of God's Church', if we are to maintain the balance and proportion of the faith. Like all the seventeenth-century Anglicans he recognized a certain primacy in the witness of the Scriptures to the original apostolic tradition, which enabled the Church to perceive if, in the course of centuries, faith or practice had gone radically out of true. In this sense, he is and remains, on the Reformation side of the sixteenth-century division. But as we have seen in the passages cited, he was aware that the appeal to Scripture alone, could leave the Christian people at the mercy of the whims and fancies of arbitrary interpretations, from whence have come so many Christian divisions. For him, therefore, the only sure way was to approach the Scriptures through the tradition, to read them in the light of the faith and worship of the Christian centuries, with the assistance of the reflection of the Fathers and Councils.[21] It is in this way that he approaches the question of the place of Mary in the scheme of redemption, and seeks to find a position of balance between the then violently opposed positions of Rome and Protestantism.

It is against this background of bitter controversy that we can best appreciate the achievement of Mark Frank's teaching on this topic. To speak of bitter controversy in this connection is no exaggeration. Passions were often violent, and feelings ran high particularly on anything to do with the veneration of Mary. One of the charges brought against Archbishop Laud at his trial was that he had caused a statue of our Lady to be put up over the porch of the university church of St Mary in Oxford. In such a context we can evaluate something of the boldness of Frank's treatment of this subject. It combines a powerful and daring eloquence with a careful and balanced judgment. While he does not hesitate to castigate the Puritan neglect of all mention of the Mother of the Lord, he also never forgets the proportion of faith, as he sees it set out in Scripture. In his sermon on the Feast of the Annunciation which contains his fullest treatment of the subject, he makes this point very clearly, and it is one which we should do well to note at the outset.

From Christ's being with her and with us, it is that we are blessed. From his incarnation begins the dawn of all our happiness. If God be not with us, all the world cannot make us happy, much less blessed. From this grace of his incarnation first riseth all our glory; so that 'Not unto us, O Lord, not unto us, but unto thy name give the praise', must she sing as well as we; and they do her wrong as well as God, that give his glory unto her, who will not give his glory to another, though to his mother, because she is but his earthly mother – a thing infinitely distant from the heavenly Father. Nor would that humble handmaid, if she should understand the vain and fond and almost idolatrous styles and honours that are given her somewhere upon earth, be pleased with them; she is highly favoured enough that her Lord and Son is with her, and she with him; she would be no higher sharer.[22]

But if Mary is never to be confused with God, always to be seen as one who draws all her grace and glory from God, she is nevertheless one who is highly, uniquely favoured, one who is, in a certain sense, the place where God is to be found, one whose childbearing stands at the very centre of the Church's life. This point is brought out very vividly in a passage from one of the sermons for Epiphany, where Frank is commenting on the coming of the Magi, who enter the house and see the young child with Mary his mother and fall down and worship him.

I do not wonder interpreters make this house the church of God. It is the gate and court of heaven, now Christ is here; angels sing round about it; all holiness is in it, now Christ is in it; here all creatures, reasonable and unreasonable, come to pay their homage to their Creator; hither they come even from the ends of the earth, to their devotions; 'a house of prayer' it is 'for all people', Gentiles and all; hither they come to worship, hither they come to pay their offerings and their vows; here is the shrine and altar, the glorious Virgin's lap, where the Saviour of the world is laid to be adored and worshipped; here stands the star for tapers to give light; and here the wise men this day become the priests – worship and offer, present prayers and praises, for themselves, and the whole world besides, all people of the world, high and low, learned and ignorant, represented by them.[22]

It is a remarkable paragraph. In the first place it shows this strong sense of the significance of the liturgical year. In the worship of the Church the mystery commemorated becomes a present reality. God is with us, in our midst. The Church's liturgy involves much more than a simple remembering of the past. Then, further, we see that his presence and manifestation among men acts as a power for reintegration, drawing together all men, all creation around this centre of light. But Mary's part is not less striking for she is at its centre; not herself the object of worship and adoration, but the altar, the shrine, the holy place where God is to be found.

Of the six sermons preached on Christmas Day, there is only one which speaks directly and at length of the role of Mary in the mystery of the incarnation, and this in itself gives an indication of the kind of proportion which Mark Frank tried to preserve. But the second sermon in which these references occur is certainly among his finest utterances. The text is Luke 2:2. 'And she brought forth her first-born son, and wrapped him in swaddling clothes, and laid him in a manger; because there was no room for them in the inn.' The sermon opens abruptly with a shout of praise and thanksgiving.

I shall not need to tell you who this 'she', or who this 'him'. The day rises with it in its wings. This day wrote it with the first ray of the morning sun upon the posts of the world. The angels sung it in their choir, the morning stars together in their courses. The Virgin Mother, the Eternal Son. The most blessed among women, the fairest of the sons of men. The woman clothed with the sun: the sun compassed with a woman. She the gate of heaven: he the King of Glory that came forth. She the mother of the everlasting God: he God without a mother; God blessed for evermore. Great persons as ever met upon a day.[24]

But as we saw in Jeremy Taylor, this greatness and glory is

hidden and not apparent. This is the theme of the whole sermon. 'Yet as great as the persons, and as great as the day, the great lesson of them both is to be little, to think and make little of ourselves; seeing the infinite greatness in this day become so little. Eternity as a child, the rays of glory wrapped in rags, Heaven crowded into the corner of a stable, and He that is everywhere want room.' The sermon is one of paradox and fruitfulness, of mysteriousness and new life, as if to emphasize that it is when the opposites come together that something new can come to birth. And what is true primarily of Mary and her Son, is true also in a measure of each one of us, for we are to 'suffer him to be born in us, who was born for us'. 'It is a day of bringing forth; sure, then, there is no being barren.'[25]

In this mysterious act, Frank says, all the unfolding of the scheme of salvation is present in little in the very beginning; '. . . the cross made up or involved in his cratch, (for of the form of a cross the cratch, some say, was made), man's salvation in God's incarnation, the Church's growth in the Virgin's bringing forth, many brethren in the First-born among them.'[26] We could hardly have a more concise statement of the way in which the whole of the economy of the Church has its roots in the childbearing of Mary. We are reminded of Andrewes's remarks about the font as the womb of the Church. And all Frank seems to say is wrapped in paradox . . . 'his Godhead in the manhood, the Word in flesh, eternity in days, righteousness in a body like to a body of sin, wisdom in the infancy of a child, abundance in poverty, glory in disrespect, the fountain of grace in a dry, barren, dusty land, eternal light in clouds, and the everlasting life in the very image of death.'[27] The Fathers themselves could not underline further the paradoxes of the incarnation and redemption.

And here all is of a piece, all follows in this sacramental way. The whole gospel, Frank maintains,

was wrapped up in clothes that seeing we might see and not presently understand, a mystery kept secret since the world began; his doctrine wrapped in parables, his grace covered in the sacraments, the inward grace in the outward elements, his great apostolic functions in poor simple fishermen, his Universal

Church in a few obscure disciples in Judaea, the height of his knowledge in the simplicity of faith, the excellency of his precepts in the plainness of his speech, and the glory of the end they drive to in the humility of the way they lead. Well may the prophet exclaim, *Vere tu es Deus absconditus*! 'Verily thou art a God that hidest thyself', O God of Israel, the Saviour![28]

As at the end of most of his festival sermons, so at the end of this one, Frank follows the example of his master, Andrewes, and applies the whole matter of his exhortation directly to the Eucharist, which is about to be celebrated, leading his hearers' attention on to the altar of the church, the place where Christ is soon to be found. Although Mary is nowhere named in this passage, we are already familiar enough with Frank's method to know that the thought of her is not far away. It is she whom we must imitate if we are to welcome Christ into the stable of our lives. This paragraph, with its evocation not only of Bethlehem but of the festivities of an English seventeenth-century Christmas, is very characteristic of its author. He is far from wishing to dissociate the sacred from the secular. He is not afraid to let heavenly mysteries be rooted even in the popular traditions of Christmas feasting, as long as they will open themselves in amazement to the overwhelming and paradoxical gratuity of God's action.

What though there be no room for him in the inn? I hope there is in our houses for him. It is Christmas time, and let us keep open house for him; let his rags be our Christmas raiment, his manger our Christmas cheer, his stable our Christmas great chamber, hall, dining room. We must clothe with him, and feed with him, and lodge with him at this feast. He is now ready by and by to give us himself to eat; you may see him wrapped ready in the swaddling clothes of his blessed sacrament; you may behold him laid upon the altar as in his manger. Do but make room for him and we will bring him forth, and you shall look upon him and handle him, and feed upon him; bring me only the rags of a rent and torn and broken and contrite heart, the white linen cloths of pure intentions and honest affections to swathe him in, wrap him up fast, and lay him close to our souls and bosoms. It is a day of mysteries: it is a mysterious business we are about; Christ wrapped up, Christ in the sacrament, Christ in a mystery; let us be content to let it go so, believe, admire and adore it.[29]

What is implicit in the sermons for Christmas and Epiphany becomes explicit in the single sermon for the Feast of the Annunciation which we must now consider. Frank takes for his text the angel's salutation; 'And the angel came in unto her and said, Hail, thou that art highly favoured, the Lord is with thee: blessed art thou among women.' In his characteristic style he begins abruptly. 'The day will tell you who this "blessed among women" is: we call it our Lady-day; and the text will tell you why she comes into the day, because the Angel came in to her. And the Angel will tell you why he today came in to her; she was "highly favoured" and "the Lord was with her", was to come himself this day in to her, to make her "the most blessed among women".'[38] As before, Frank chooses to make use of the popular name for the feast, Lady-day, in order to begin his exposition of its meaning; like Andrewes he enjoys teasing out the different meanings of simple phrases, drawing his doctrine from elementary forms of speech, preaching, we may suppose, to a congregation in which people of very different levels of education were gathered.

His whole exposition here is centred upon the words *Dominus tecum*, 'The Lord is with thee'. Everything either follows from it, or leads towards it. Even the apparently incidental fact that the feast falls in Lent, and that this might seem inappropriate, is seen in this context. With a sharp intuition into the value of fasting, he says, 'It is the very time for *gratia plena*, to be filled when we are empty; the only time for *Dominus tecum*, for our Lord's being with us, when we have most room to entertain him.'[31] It is when man knows himself to be poor and empty that God can come. As he remarks later in the sermon, 'It was the humility of his handmaid that God, in this high favour of the Incarnation of his Son, respected in her. Humility the ground of all grace within us – all grace without us, – of God's grace to us, – of his grace in us – the very grace that graces them all.'[32] Mary's blessedness, her glory, lies above all things in her humility. She points us always to the one who comes to her, who comes in her. It is this which enables the preacher to maintain that balance or proportion of faith, which he so much admires and which he feels is threatened both by those who disparage or ignore her, and by those whose veneration for her runs to an exaggeration which defeats its own ends.

Indeed *Dominus tecum* is the chief business; the Lord Christ's being with her, that which the Church especially commemorates in the day. Her being 'blessed' and all our being 'blessed', 'highly favoured', or favoured at all, either men or women being so, all our hail, all our health and peace and joy, all the angels' visits to us, or kind words, all our conferences with heaven, all our titles and honours in heaven and earth, that are worth naming, come only from it. For *Dominus tecum* cannot come without them; he cannot come to us but we must be so, must be highly favoured in it, and blessed by it. So the Incarnation of Christ, and the Annunciation of the Blessed Virgin – his being incarnate of her, and her blessedness by him, all our blessedness in him with her, make it as well our Lord's as our Lady's day. More his, because his being Lord made her a Lady, else a poor carpenter's wife, God knows; all her worthiness and honour, as all ours, is from him; and we to take heed today, or any day, of parting them; or so remembering her as to forget him; or so blessing her as to take away any of our blessing him; and of his worship to give to her. Let her blessedness, the respect we give her, be *inter mulieres*, 'among women' still; such as is fit and proportionate to weak creatures, not due and proper only to the Creator, that *Dominus tecum*, Christ in her be the business: that we take pattern by the Angel, to give her no more than is due to her, yet to be sure to give her that though, and that particularly upon the day.[33]

Frank is well aware of the difficulties of his theme. In the context of his own time in which the subject had been one of such violent controversy, there was much to be said for leaving it in silence. Indeed he may also have felt a deeper reason for reticence before this mystery, a sense that here are subjects which are fit more for inner meditation than for public exposition. Yet it is the very needs of his time which force him to speak out. Where the faith is distorted or exaggerated, ignored or derided, it is necessary to try

68

to restore the balance, and to find the true proportion. And this point about the Mother of the Lord which is apparently a secondary one, is in fact intimately related to the very heart of the Christian affirmation, that God and man are reconciled in Christ.

Nor should I scarce, I confess, have chosen such a theme today, though the Gospel reach it me, but that I see it is time to do it, when our Lord is wounded through our Lady's sides, both our Lord and the mother of our Lord, most vilely spoken of by a new generation of wicked men, who, because the Romanists make little less of her than a goddess, they make not so much of her as a good woman; because they bless her too much, these unbless her quite, at least will not suffer her to be blessed as she should.[34]

In dealing with this subject, Frank then closely follows the text of St Luke, basing all his exposition on that, but at the same time turning for guidance to the Fathers. In this case it is the more remarkable that he does so because he may himself have felt uneasy at some of the ways in which they develop the theme. As before, it is not only the early Fathers who are cited, but also St Bernard (or at least sermons then attributed to him), St Peter Damian and Hugh of St Victor. In this he simply follows the practice of Lancelot Andrewes, who frequently cites St Bernard alongside the teachers of the fourth century. If Frank felt any reserves about some aspects of their Mariology, he says nothing of them in the course of the sermon, but quotes them as authorities together with St Jerome and St Ambrose.

We find recurring in the sermon many of the themes with which we are already familiar in Andrewes and Taylor. There is for instance the comparison of Mary with the angels. Having spoken of Gabriel, the angel of the annunciation, and given various patristic interpretations of the meaning of his name, Frank says: 'So we have done with him; come we now to her – a greater than he – if we may speak with Epiphanius and some others.'[35] Or again there is the thought of Mary as the type and model of the life of contemplation; 'If we look for angels' company and salutations, we must be much within. 'A garden enclosed is my sister, my spouse; a spring shut up, a fountain sealed,' says Christ. The spouse of

Christ, the soul he loves and vouchsafes his company, much private, oft within – within and at her prayers and meditation too. So was the blessed Virgin (say the Fathers here), blessedly employed, watching at her devotions. . .'[36] In both cases, if we are to find the language more than picturesque and baffling we must reflect on all that the inner journey of man involves, the hazards and the achievements; and must consider that the central affirmation of the union of God with man in Christ implies that none of the forces of the inner or the outer world, however apparently powerful they may be, can separate us from the love of God in Christ. In the union of man with God in Christ something of still greater significance has occurred. Only in the light of the redemptive incarnation can we begin to see the meaning of this tradition about the service of the angels.

So the preacher comes to the terms of the angelic salutation: Hail, Ave. 'It speaks joy and peace and health, and salvation, both to her, and to us by her. . .'[37] for we all are involved in this salutation. He examines in detail the meaning of Gabriel's form of address. He assures us that he will not give Mary styles and titles other than those contained in Scripture; there is to be no equalling her with God. But at the same time, we are not to think simply to equal her with ourselves, however much we may remember her sharing our creatureliness.

We are not to salute great persons by their names, but by their titles; and the Mother of God is above the greatest we meet with upon earth. We must not be too familiar with those whom God so highly favours; that is our lesson hence. We are not to speak of the Blessed Virgin, the Apostles and Saints, as if we were speaking to our servants, Paul, Peter, Mary or the like. It is a new fashion of religion, neither taken from saints, nor angels, nor any of heaven or heavenly spirits, to unsaint the saints, to deny them their proper titles, to level them with the meanest of our servants.[38]

Again he turns to the Fathers, to fill out his interpretation. The name Mary is 'high and illustrious', he tells us.

Maria is *maris stella*, says St Bede: 'the star of the sea'; a fit name

70

for the mother of the bright Morning Star that rises out of the vast sea of God's infinite and endless love. Maria, the Syriac interprets *domina*, 'a lady', a name yet retained and given to her by all Christians; our Lady, or the Lady Mother of our Lord. Maria, rendered by Petrus Damiani, *de monte et altitudine Dei*, highly exalted as you would say, like the mountain of God, in which he would vouchsafe to dwell, after a more miraculous manner than in very Sion, his 'own holy mount'. St Ambrose interprets it, *Deus ex genere meo*, 'God of my kin'; as if by her very name she was designed to have God born of her, to be *deipara*, as the Church, against all heretics, has ever styled her the Mother of God.[39]

It is in this context that, having earlier affirmed the solidarity between Mary and all believers, he can also confidently assert the uniqueness of her calling, a uniqueness which yet includes us all within itself.

He is not with her, as he is with any else. *Tecum in mente, tecum in ventre*, as the Fathers gloss it; *Tecum in spiritu, tecum in carne*, with her he was, or would be presently, as well in her body as in her soul, personally, essentially, nay bodily with her, and take a body from her – a way of being with any never heard before or since, – a being with her beyond any expression or conception whatsoever. And the Lord thus being with her, all good must needs be with her: all gracious ways of his being with us are comprehended in it; so the salutation no way exceeded. And well may he choose to be with her – even make haste and prevent the Angel, as St Bernard speaks, to be with her. He is with 'the pure in heart', with the humble spirit and piously retired soul, and she is all.[2]

From the theological point of view, one of the most interesting passages in the sermon is that where he discusses the meaning of the words *gratia plena*: 'highly favoured', 'full of grace'. The two translations sum up in themselves one of the crucial controversies of the sixteenth and seventeenth centuries. Is God's grace his unmerited favour towards us, *favor Dei*, or is it a supernatural gift which he implants in us, *gratia infusa*? As we have seen, it is fundamental to Frank's position that all the blessedness of Mary is of God's pure gift. It is noteworthy that he nowhere in this sermon uses the language of 'merit'. In this sense he belongs to the Reformation side of the controversy. Grace is not primarily a quality which we possess. It is the name for a relationship initiated by God. But to say this is not necessarily to deny the other interpretation, for this relationship with God is a transforming relationship, which creates anew the one who is drawn into it. So we find that Frank refuses to recognize a necessary opposition between the two approaches. Having assured the primacy of God's action, he happily equates the two. ' "Thou that art highly favoured", so our new translation renders it: "full of grace"; so our old hath it, from the Latin, *gratia plena*; and both right; for it will carry both. Grace is favour; God's grace is divine favour; high in grace, high in his favour; full of his grace, full of his favour, – all comes to one.'[41] It is a remarkable affirmation in face of the bitter controversies of the time.

Where he is concerned to make distinctions is between 'sanctifying and edifying' grace, 'the gifts of the Holy Spirit that sanctify and make us holy; or the gifts that make us serviceable to make others so.' Here he is anxious to reject a view which will give Mary so much as to take her totally out of the human context, which will make it impossible to compare her with other saints. Like Taylor he insists that she has her own proper excellence, but not the excellence of others.

> Of each kind she had her fullness according to her measure, and the designation that God appointed her. For sanctifying graces, none fuller, *solo Deo excepto*, 'God only excepted', saith Epiphanius. And it is fit enough to believe that she who was so highly honoured to have her womb filled with the body of the Lord, had her soul as fully filled by the Holy Ghost.
>
> For edifying graces, as they came not all into her measure, she was not to preach, to administer, to govern, to play the apostle, and therefore no necessity she should be full of all those gifts, being those are not distributed all to any, but . . . to everyone according to his measure and employment. . . Where any edifying grace was necessary for her, she had it as well as others;

more perhaps than others. When it was not necessary, it was no way to the impairing of her fullness, though she had it not.[42]

As we might expect from Frank's treatment of the idea of blessing which we have already seen, it is when he comes to speak of Mary as blessed that his eloquence reaches its fullest pitch. It is a passage which is interesting in many ways. Considered biblically, it combines Old and New Testament allusions, the blessings promised to faithful Israel in Deuteronomy 28, together with a reference to the crucial verses, Luke 11:27–28, where in reply to the woman who cries out 'Blessed is the womb that bore thee', Jesus declares, 'Yea, rather blessed are they who hear the word of God and keep it.' They are interpreted here as the Evangelist surely meant them to be, as not pointing away from Mary, but to the true nature of her blessedness who 'kept all these things and pondered them in her heart'. At the same time, and by way of the Old Testament, the passage takes up the idea of the fruitfulness of creation, the good earth open to God's grace and mercy which shower down from heaven upon it. The notion of man as a microcosm has a very special relevance here, for Mary may be seen as herself the land of promise, at the heart and centre of the creation, as it turns itself towards God. The circling of the seasons as well as the history of God's choice of a particular people find their fulfilment in her bringing forth. 'All creation rejoices in thee', the Eastern Church sings to the Mother of God. Mark Frank in his preaching makes the affirmation no less clearly.

From this follows the second title, 'blessed', blessed of God, blessed of man; blessed in the city, and blessed in the field. Cities and countries call her blessed; blessed in the fruit of her body, in her blessed child Jesus. Blessed in the fruit of her ground, her cattle, her kine, and her sheep, in the inferior faculties of her soul and body; all fructify to Christ. Blessed her basket and her store, her womb and her breasts; the womb that bare him, and the paps that gave him suck. Blessed in her going out and her coming in, the Lord still being with her; the good treasure of heaven still open to her, showering down upon her, and the earth filled with the blessings which she brought forth into the world, when she brought forth the Son of God. Blessed she indeed that was the conduit of so great blessings, though blessed most in the bearing him in her soul, much more than bearing him in her body. So Christ intimates to the woman that began to 'bless the womb', that is, the mother 'that bare him'; 'Yea rather,' says he, 'blessed they that hear the word of God and keep it'; as if he had said, She is more blessed in bearing the word in her soul than in her body.[43]

We feel, in such a passage, how much our Christianity has lost by not being truly rooted in the material order, by not allowing the feminine, receptive side of our humanity to enter fully into our mode of experience and our manner of thought. Frank opens to us the possibility of reappropriating part of the tradition, and, what is more, part of ourselves. The whole creation of which we are part can become for us the burning bush, on fire with the glory of the divinity yet not consumed, as we learn to receive it wholly as the gift of God. It is precisely because he sees Mary at the centre of this creation that Frank puts an absolute negative against any temptation to translate her to the side of the Creator. Her blessedness is full, but it is always 'a blessedness compatible to the creature'.

So once again he cautions against a distorted attitude towards her, seeking to find the true proportion of faith.

Give we her in God's name the honour due to her. God hath styled her 'blessed' by the angel, by Elizabeth; commanded all generations to call her so, and they hitherto hath done it, and let us do it too. Indeed some of late have overdone it; yet let us not therefore underdo it, but do it as we hear the angel and the first Christians did it; account of her and speak of her as the most blessed among women, one 'highly favoured', most 'highly' too. But all the while give *Dominus tecum*, all the glory, the whole glory of all to him; give her the honour and blessedness of the chief of saints, – him only the glory that she is so, and that by her conceiving and bringing our Saviour into the world we are made heirs, and shall one day be partakers of the blessedness she enjoys, when the Lord shall be with us too, and we need no angel to tell us so.[44]

It is in relation to the coming of Christ that Mary's glory is truly to be seen. And she who stands at the centre of creation stands also at the centre of the company of those who believe, as in the Eastern icons of the ascension and Pentecost she is seen standing in the midst of the apostolic band. She is the type of every Christian in whom the Lord is to be born,

> especially if we now here dispose ourselves by chastity, humility, and devotion, as she did, to receive him, and let him be new born in us. The pure and virgin soul, the humble spirit, the devout affection will be also highly favoured; the Lord be with them and bless them above others. Blessed is the virgin soul, more blessed than others in St Paul's opinion; blessed the humble spirit above all. For God hath exalted the humble and meek, the humble handmaid better than the proudest lady. Blessed the devout affection that is always watching for her Lord in prayer and meditations; none so happy, so blessed as she; the Lord comes to none so soon as such.

It is some measure of the imbalance of male and female elements within us, and in our society, that we may feel a certain unease to find that for Frank these virtues of the woman should have necessarily to characterize *all* who believe in God. The vision of Christ as our mother, which occurs so naturally in Julian of Norwich, the expectation that men should feel a motherly tenderness towards one another, which we find in St Francis, or the early Cistercian writers, such things demand a situation in which it is accepted that everyone carries the male and the female, *animus* and *anima*, within himself and that any fullness of life demands their reconciliation. It is a vision which we greatly need to rediscover, and which much now urges us to find again for our health and the health of our whole society. Frank at least is quite clear on this point in his final affirmation.

In the concluding paragraphs of his sermon where he turns directly to the Eucharist, he prays that 'we also may become Marys, and the mothers of our Lord'. In this final section we can see something of a coming together of all the themes we have been studying; Christ's presence in the flesh through the childbearing of blessed Mary, is the foundation of his presence in the Church, in each Christian, and in the Holy Communion, which thus becomes the focal point of the mystery of God's presence among his people, the centre of celebration for man and for all things.

The Lord comes, he declares, to none

> more fully than in the blessed Sacrament to which we are now a-going. There he is strangely with us, highly favours us, exceeding blesses us; there we are all made blessed Marys, and become mothers, sisters, and brothers of our Lord, while we hear his word, and conceive it in us; while we believe him who is the Word, and receive him too into us. There angels come to us on heavenly errands, and there our Lord indeed is with us, and we are blessed, and the angels hovering all about us to peep into those holy mysteries, think us so, call us so. There graces pour down in abundance on us – there grace is in its fullest plenty – there his highest favours are bestowed upon us – there we are filled with grace unless we hinder it, and shall hereafter in the strength of it be exalted into glory – there to sit down with this blessed Virgin and all the saints and angels, and sing praise, and honour, and glory, to him, Father, Son and Holy Ghost, for ever and ever.[45]

NOTES

1 Mark Frank, *Sermons*, Library of Anglo-Catholic Theology, vol. ii, p. 123
2 Ibid., i, p. 300
3 Ibid., ii, pp. 123–4
4 Aelred Squire, *Asking the Fathers*, (1973), p. 56
5 A. L. Maycock, *Chronicles of Little Gidding* (London 1954), p. 3
6 Ibid., i, pp. 340–1
7 Ibid., i, p. 5
8 Ibid., i, p. 191
9 Ibid., i, p. 192
10 Ibid., i, p. 55
11 Ibid., i, p. 223
12 Ibid., ii, p. 301
13 Ibid., i, p. 139
14 Ibid., i, p. 158–9
15 Ibid., i, pp. 381–2
16 Ibid., i, p. 126

17   Ibid., i, p. 126
18   Ibid., ii, p. 115
19   Ibid., ii, p. 234
20   Ibid., ii, p. 235
21   For an interesting study of the way in which Lancelot Andrewes
      handles this theme in his preaching see the article by Nicholas Lossky,
      'La patristique dans la prédication anglaise au début du xviie siècle:
      un exemple, Lancelot Andrewes', in *Messager de l'exarchat du patri-
      arche russe en Europe occidentale*, nos. 105–8 (1980–81), pp. 113–21.
22   Op. cit., ii, pp. 48–9
23   Ibid., i, p. 280
24   Ibid., i, p. 77
25   Ibid., i, pp. 89–91
26   Ibid., i, p. 86
27   Ibid., i, p. 86
28   Ibid., i. p. 87
29   Ibid., i, p. 90
30   Ibid., ii, p. 33
31   Ibid., ii, p. 34
32   Ibid., ii, p. 48
33   Ibid., ii, p. 34
34   Ibid., ii, pp. 35–6
35   Ibid., ii, p. 39
36   Ibid., ii, p. 41
37   Ibid., ii, p. 42
38   Ibid., ii, p. 45
39   Ibid., ii, pp. 32–40
40   Ibid., ii, pp. 43–4
41   Ibid., ii, pp. 45–6
42   Ibid., ii, p. 46
43   Ibid., ii, pp. 47–8
44   Ibid., ii, p. 50
45   Ibid., ii, pp. 50–51

4

'The Whole Assembly Sings': Thomas Traherne

We have examined so far the work of three seventeenth-century theologians, and sought to trace in them a number of closely related themes; the union of God and man in Christ, its celebration in the Church's liturgy, the redemption of the whole of human nature, and what this means in particular for the redemption of the body, and the place of Mary in this whole complex mystery. We must now look to another writer from a little later in the same century, in whom these different but related themes find a final and startling treatment. Final, because already in the years after the restoration of the monarchy the philosophical and scientific presuppositions which had made it possible to regard man as a microcosm were rapidly collapsing; startling, because here we are dealing with a writer with a peculiarly personal vision, and an ecstatic and incomparable style in which to convey it. Thomas Traherne was not a professional theologian and teacher as were Andrewes, Taylor and Frank. He was to outward appearances an undistinguished clergyman, first, incumbent of a small parish near Hereford, then private chaplain to an influential courtier. Inwardly he was a man of vision, a poet alike in his prose and verse. He was not concerned so much to set out the pattern of Christian faith as a whole as to witness to his own particular vision of things; his astonishing recollection of the childhood experience of eternity and his sense of man's felicity in the world, when the world is perceived as God's creation. It would be a mistake, however, to suppose that Traherne is concerned only with his private vision. In the *Centuries of Medita-*

78

tions and the *Christian Ethics*, he shows himself a man of learning, and an inheritor of the theological tradition which we have been describing. He also has read deeply in the Fathers. Although he develops the themes with which we are concerned in a highly personal way, it is striking that in him they are interconnected exactly as they are in Andrewes, in Taylor or in Frank.

In his own time, Traherne was virtually unknown. The things that he was saying and the way in which he was saying them were already becoming old-fashioned, almost anachronistic by the time of his death in 1674. Indeed it is only in our own century that Traherne has won a secure if minor place within the history of English literature. The writer whose description of childhood ecstasy most closely resembles that of Wordsworth was wholly unknown in the lifetime of Wordsworth. Of the texts which we shall quote none was published before our own century, and one was first published in 1970. With Traherne, the themes with which we are concerned are already ceasing to be the primary concern of theologians. They are beginning to pass into the hands of the poets.

Whereas the writings which we have been dealing with in previous chapters have been little known and relatively inaccessible, some of the great passages in Traherne's *Centuries of Meditations* have become rightly famous and have passed into innumerable anthologies. Traherne's vision is his own, but his idea of man as created in God's image, rejoicing in all that God has made, is not in its substance very different from that which we find in Mark Frank. Inward and outward unite in the praise of God:

> You never enjoy the world aright, till the sea itself floweth in your veins, till you are clothed with the heavens, and crowned with the stars; and perceive yourself to be the sole heir of the whole world; and more than so, because men are in it who are every one sole heirs as well as you. Till you can sing and rejoice and delight in God, as misers do in gold, and kings in sceptres, you never enjoy the world.[1]

But what is often not recognized is that this sense of coinherence with the world has as its presupposition the faith that man is created in God's image, and that this image is restored and re-established

79

in Christ. Contrary to the impression which many people have, Traherne's religion is not simply one of joy in creation. The theme of redemption appears powerfully in it, as a reading of the central chapters of the first *Century* shows.

> Would men consider what God hath done, they would be ravished in Spirit with the glory of his doings. For heaven and earth are full of the majesty of his glory. And how happy would men be could they see and enjoy it. But above all these our Saviour's cross is the throne of delights. That centre of eternity, that tree of life in the midst of the paradise of God. . . The cross of Christ is the Jacob's ladder by which we ascend into the highest heavens. There we see joyful patriarchs, expectant saints and prophets ministering, apostles publishing and doctors teaching. All nations concentring and angels praising. That cross is a tree set on fire with the invisible flame that illuminateth all the world. The flame is Love. The love in his bosom who died on it. In the light of which we see how to possess all the things in heaven and earth after his similitude.[2]

We should therefore greatly misunderstand Traherne if we thought of him simply as a solitary visionary. While he celebrates the inner riches of man's life restored in God, in harmony with all created things, he is not unaware that this life has its outward social aspect, that things inward and outward are to rejoice together. So we can find in him, no less than in Andrewes and Frank, a celebration of the feast of Christ's nativity in which personal and social are joined together into one. In fact, in his poem 'Christmas-Day' we might say that something of the old undivided unity of Christendom, inward and outward, rich and poor, the world of nature and the world of man, Church and state together, finds expression, and Hereford becomes for an instant the image of the city, as the bells of the parish churches ring through the December air, and the mayor proceeds in state into the cathedral.

> See how, their bodies clad with finer clothes,
>   They now begin
>   His praise to sing
> Who purchas'd their repose:

Whereby their inward joy they do disclose:
Their dress alludes to better works than those;
   His gayer weeds and finer band,
   New suit and hat, into his hand
   The Plow-man takes, his neatest shoes,
   And warmer gloves, he means to use:
      And shall not I, my king
      Thy praises sing.

See how their breath doth smoke, and how they haste
      His praise to sing
      With cherubim;
   They scarce a breakfast taste;
But through the streets, lest precious time should waste,
When service doth begin, to church they haste
      And shall not I, Lord, come to thee,
      The beauty of thy temple see?
      Thy name with joy I will confess,
      Clad in my Saviour's righteousness
       'Mong all thy servants sing
         To thee my king.

'Twas thou that gav'st us cause for fine attires;
      Ev'n thou, O King,
      As in the spring,
      Dost warm us with thy fires
Of love; thy blood hath bought us new desires
Thy righteousness doth clothe with new attires.
      Made fresh and fine let me appear
      This day divine, to close the year;
      Among the rest let me be seen
      A living branch and always green,
       Think it a pleasant thing
         Thy praise to sing.

At break of day, O how the bells did ring!
      To thee, my King
      The bells did ring;
   To thee the angels sing;

Thy goodness did produce this other spring,
For this it is they make the bells to ring:
    The sounding bells do through the air
    Proclaim thy welcome far and near;
    While I alone with thee inherit
       All these joys, beyond my merit.
       Who would not always sing
        To such a King?

I, all these joys, above my merit, see
      By thee, my King,
      To whom I sing
    Entire, convey'd to me.
My treasure, Lord, thou mak'st the people be
That I with pleasure might thy servants see.
    Ev'n in their rude external ways
    They do set forth my Saviour's praise,
    And minister a light to me;
    While I by them do hear to thee
    Praises, my Lord and King,
      Whole churches sing.

Hark how remoter parishes do sound!
    Far off they ring
    For thee, my King,
    Ev'n round about the town;
The churches scattered over all the ground
Serve for thy praise, who art with glory crown'd.
    This city is an engine great
    That makes my pleasure more complete
    The sword, the mace, the magistrate
    To honour thee, attend in state
      The whole assembly sings;
       The Minster rings.[3]

The poem is, as we say, an almost physical embodiment of what it is seeking to describe; the celebration of Christ's coming on the part of a whole Christian people. All the objects named in it play their part in the unity of the whole. But however fine the poetic achievement, we cannot overlook the deeply felt and understood theology which underlies it. Christmas is the celebration of Christ's nativity, therefore of the unity of man with God in him. In the darkness and cold of man's alienation from God and from his neighbour, a new and 'mid-winter' spring appears. The coldness of man's frozen perceptions is warmed by the love of God, new desires arise in his heart and are guided by the divine wisdom. He is drawn into unity with himself. And this inward unity and rejoicing must express itself outwardly; and it does so in material things, in hats and gloves and newly polished shoes, in eager last-minute attempts to get to church on time. As in the sermons of Mark Frank, so here, the unity of inward and outward is complete. The whole method is one of sacramental presentation. Here in the midst of the congregation, the eucharistic assembly of Christmas, the praises of men are united with those of the angels around the coming together of heaven and earth.

One of the most striking features of the poem is its use of clanging rhythms and constantly recurring rhyme words to suggest the effect of change-ringing, at that time a comparatively new practice. The bells become central to the scene. The two poems which stand next after this one in Traherne's manuscript, also have bells as their theme; hard metallic objects, which can yet sound out in the praise of God and summon men to worship him.

> Their iron tongues
> Do utter songs
> And shall our stony hearts make no reply?

Made of the things of earth, of the most base things, yet they can announce heavenly joys to those who hear them.

> Doth not each trembling sound I hear
> Make all my spirits dance?
> Each stroke's a message to my ear
> That casts my soul into a trance
> Of joy . . .

But bells to ring out clear and true must be whole and uncracked, and so we too must find unity and integrity.

        We must unite
        If we delight
    Would yield or feel, or any excellence.[4]

Each man, as Traherne at all times likes to insist, since he sums
up within himself the whole creation, enjoys this celebration whole
and entire. All things are ours, not just collectively, but in some
more mysterious way, personally. This is part of what it means
that man is made in the image of God; that each human person is
unique, and each a created fullness. And as all things come together
into God, so all the steeples with their clashing bells unite in one,
and call men together into God's service. The whole city, the
complex articulation of man's social life, becomes an icon of the
praise of God, a reflection of his glory.

Traherne's poetry, even at its best, does not often arrive at the
same quality of ecstasy as is to be found in the finest of his prose.
But it is noteworthy that this poem which celebrates the feast of
Christ's nativity recapitulates themes and images which come in
one of the most dazzling of all the *Meditations*, the third chapter
of the third *Century*. In this vision of childhood, as contrasted
with that of Wordsworth or Edwin Muir, for example, the city is
not absent. Rather it is the juxtaposition of town and country, of
man and nature, which is so striking. In the moment of vision all
things come together into one.

> . . . All things abided eternally as they were in their proper
> places. Eternity was manifest in the light of day, and something
> infinite behind everything appeared; which talked with my
> expectation and moved my desire. The city seemed to stand in
> Eden, or to be built in heaven. The streets were mine, the temple
> was mine, the people were mine, their clothes and gold and silver
> were mine, as much as their sparkling eyes, fair skins and ruddy
> faces.[5]

The initial moment of vision faded, but it would be reaffirmed in
adult life, in the context of a faith in the incarnation and redemption. Here again eternity shines through the things of time, and
material objects become vehicles of the divine glory. After experience and suffering it is possible, in the strength of the incarnation

84

and redemption, to affirm again, at a greater depth and with a greater compassion, the primal vision of infancy.

All this is latent within the poem on 'Christmas', and it is clear that something very precious has found expression in it. It seems to embody and show forth the significance of the sacred city as it had been seen and known in medieval East and West alike. It forms a late representation of unities which had found embodiment throughout Christendom, in Novgorod or Mistra, in Chartres or Siena, in Canterbury or Hereford. It seems as if, in the seventeenth century when these unities were beginning to fall apart, men had a last and particularly vivid perception of them. Aelred Squire in *Asking the Fathers* remarks on this in connection with one of the royal houses in Copenhagen. The Rosenborg Slot he maintains, 'from many points of view, like much of the art of the incredibly fertile mid-seventeenth century, is almost a physical embodiment of the thought and feeling of an age that was still in vital contact with many of the common insights of the medieval world. These insights are often clearer and easier to grasp for us today in their late-received form than in their older originals.'[6] This is certainly true here, and it sheds light on the special attraction of the seventeenth-century poets for our own day.

We might have expected that Traherne, with his sharp perception of the presence of God as made known in material things, would have given some special attention to the place of the body in man's spiritual life, and this is precisely what we find. The first of the thanksgivings published shortly after his death is a Thanksgiving for the Body, in which Traherne enumerates in detail the parts of the body and the qualities of the physical world. In the concluding prayer he writes: 'I give thee thanks for the being thou givest unto the heavens, sun, moon, stars and elements; to beasts, plants and all other bodies of the earth, to the fowls of the air, the fishes of the sea. I give thee thanks for the beauty of colours, for the harmony of sounds, for the pleasantness of odours, for the sweetness of meats, for the warmth and softness of our raiment, and for all my five senses, and all the pores of my body. . .'[7] We might further have thought that it would be probable that in him, as in the earlier writers we have considered, such a way of appreciating the faith might have led to some particular meditation upon Mary.

The publication in December 1970 of a devotion to our Lady, hitherto existing only in manuscript, proves that this also is the case. It is so fine a piece of writing that it demands to be quoted in full.

> And first O Lord I praise and magnify thy Name
> For the Most Holy Virgin-Mother of God, who is the Highest
>   of thy Saints.
> The most Glorious of all thy Creatures.
> The most Perfect of all thy Works.
> The nearest unto Thee, in the Throne of God.
>   Whom Thou didst please to make
> Daughter of the Eternal Father.
> Mother of the Eternal Son.
> Spouse of the Eternal Spirit.
> Tabernacle of the most Glorious Trinity.
> Mother of Jesus.
> Mother of the Messias.
> Mother of Him who was the Desire of all Nations.
> Mother of the Prince of Peace.
> Mother of the King of Heaven.
> Mother of our Creator.
> Mother and Virgin.
> Mirror of Humility and Obedience.
> Mirror of Wisdom and Devotion.
> Mirror of Modesty and Chastity.
> Mirror of Sweetness and Resignation.
> Mirror of Sanctity.
> Mirror of all virtues.
> The most Illustrious Light in the Church, Wearing over all her
>   Beauties the veil of Humility to shine the more resplendently
>   in thy Eternal Glory.
>
> And yet this Holy Virgin-Mother styled herself but the
>   Handmaid of the Lord, and falls down with all the Glorious
>   Hosts of Angels, and with the Armies of Saints, at the foot
>   of Thy Throne, to worship and Glorify Thee for ever and
>   ever.

I praise Thee O Lord with all the Powers and faculties of my
Soul; for doing in Her all thy Merciful Works for my sake,
and the Benefit of Mankind. For uttering the Glorious Word:
yea rather Blessed are they that Hear the Word of God,
and Keep it. And for looking round about upon Thy
Disciples and saying, Behold my Mother and my Brethren.
For whosoever shall do the Will of God, the same is my
Brother and my Sister and Mother. Yea for what thou wilt
say, Inasmuch as ye have done it to the least of these, ye
have done it unto me.

The most unworthy of all thy Servants falleth down to worship
Thee for thine own Excellencies; even Thee O Lord, for
thine own perfection, and for all those Glorious Graces,
given and imparted to this Holy Virgin, and to all thy
Saints.[8]

In the article with which he introduced and published this text,
J. E. Barnes discussed the question of its authorship and purpose.
He considered the possibility that Traherne might have copied it
into his book of meditations from some other source. He looked
at the hypothesis that it might have been intended to be used as a
litany, each of the titles in the first section to have been followed
by the words 'pray for us'.

As to the first point, it would seem to me virtually certain that
the devotion is Traherne's. The style is his, and as we have seen,
the content is completely in harmony with his way of seeing things.
It is true, as Barnes points out, that much of the language has no
exact parallel in seventeenth-century Anglican writing, but a careful
examination of its contents shows that it is substantially in accord
with the tradition which stems from Hooker and Andrewes, which
we have been examining. At least this is so, as long as we resolve
the point of its intended use, by deciding that the devotion was
not intended as a litany, and that the various titles of our Lady
which it gives are all governed by the words 'whom thou didst
make'. Seen in this light, the whole text forms one single act
of prayer and praise addressed to God, in which the thankful
commemoration of the Virgin is included.

Read thus, the theological balance of the meditation is remarkable. Traherne begins by praising and magnifying God for the Blessed Virgin. The words used at once suggest forms of prayers, which though they did not occur in the English Book of Common Prayer of 1662, had a certain liturgical authority for Anglicans from their use in the 1549 Prayer Book, and in John Cosin's *Book of Hours*. If in his meditation he is going to go beyond what is customary in the Church, he chooses to begin with what is commonly accepted. Traherne, indeed, does at once go on to ascribe to Mary titles and honours which have never had a place in official Anglican formularies. Barnes points to a poem of Ben Jonson's in which our Lady is spoken of as 'Daughter and Mother and the Spouse of God', and also to some verses of Bishop Ken dating from the end of the century, in which similar language is used. But, as he says, such examples are exceptional, and the terms of the first lines of Traherne's text go beyond what we might expect, even in a writer like Frank. However, when we come to the series of 'Mother' and 'Mirror' titles we may be surprised at their discretion. The first group are all either scriptural or closely related to Scripture; the second insist upon Mary as the mirror of humility and obedience, those specific qualities, for which, as we have seen, she is commended by other seventeenth-century Anglican writers. The very beautiful phrase which occurs in the last line of this section, 'wearing over all her beauties the veil of humility', suggests a reminiscence of Taylor's phrase, 'those graces that walk in a veil and silence', or Frank's description of her humility as 'the grace that graces them all'. It is in her humility that her true greatness is to be found.

Then having celebrated the greatness of 'this Holy Virgin-Mother', with beautiful and splendid titles, Traherne goes on to say, '*And yet . . .*' reminding himself that Mary's greatness is in her lowliness, and that she is one who with all angels and saints falls down in worship before the throne of God. The dialectical movement of thought here is similar to that which we have seen in Mark Frank. He, having spoken of the height of Mary's calling, yet reminds us that her blessedness is always a blessedness 'compatible to the creature'. The following paragraph in Traherne takes up again the initial act of praise, addressed to God and not to Mary, for all that he has done in Mary and above all for the promise that all who hear the word of God and keep it shall have a share in her blessedness. Again the themes which we have seen before are present; the words of the gospel are explicitly recalled, it is made clear that Mary stands as a model for all who believe, 'the most illustrious light *in* the Church'. Finally the writer praises God for what he is in himself, and for all his gifts given to the Blessed Virgin and all the saints, and with them falls silent before the mystery of God in Trinity.

In the light of our investigation of seventeenth-century Anglican Mariology, it is difficult not to feel a certain joy at the publication of this text. On the one hand it has an exuberance, a freedom, a directness, which is not often found in Anglican writing about Mary, from whatever century it comes. It seems remarkably unanxious, unpolemical. In this sense it can stand beside some of the great classical texts of Marian devotion of East and West alike. On the other hand, it reveals a balance and a judgement which is not always present in devotional writing, whatever its subject. The praise of Mary is contained within the greater praise of God, to whom alone all worship is due. Traherne the poet and the visionary is at one with Traherne the theologian.

NOTES
1 Thomas Traherne, *Poems, Centuries and Three Thanksgivings* ed. Anne Ridler (Oxford 1966), p. 177
2 Ibid., pp. 189–191
3 Ibid., pp. 100–103
4 Ibid., pp. 104–5
5 Ibid., p. 264
6 Aelred Squire, *Asking the Fathers* (1973), p. 10
7 Op. cit., pp. 388–9
8 *Theology*, vol. lxxiii, no. 606 (December 1970), J. E. Barnes, 'A Caroline Devotion to the Virgin Mary', pp. 535–41

Part Two

Transition

5

From Ken to Heber

It would be a mistake to suppose that the distinctive theological and spiritual tradition which we have been examining so far came to an end at the close of the seventeenth century. There are signs that its influence continued to be felt throughout the period which followed, until, in the middle of the nineteenth century, the Oxford Movement gave a fresh impetus to the Anglican quest for catholicity. But the change in intellectual and cultural atmosphere which took place towards the end of the seventeenth century, a change represented in science by the early leaders of the Royal Society, in literature by the work of men like Addison and Pope, and in the Church by an Archbishop such as Tillotson, certainly brought with it great changes in the world of theology and spirituality. The old confident assertion of a correspondence between man and nature which had marked the earlier seventeenth century could no longer be maintained. The picture of man as microcosm no longer carried weight. The former highly metaphorical style of writing and preaching gave way to a plainer, more directly rational form of discourse. The minds of the theologians turned away from the study of the Fathers, which had been so characteristic both of England and of France in the seventeenth century. New and very different ways of approach were adopted.

In the Church of England this change was hastened by the schism of the non-jurors which took place following the revolution of 1689. Among the clergy who refused to take the oath of allegiance to William III were many of the most learned and conscientious of the high-churchmen. Although the non-juring body was never very large it contained for a time distinguished figures whom the established Church could ill afford to lose. Outstanding among these was Thomas Ken, Bishop of Bath and Wells, already in his own day respected everywhere as a man of notable holiness of life. Ken was not a scholar; in fact he wrote relatively little in prose. His output of verse is considerably larger, but it must be confessed that on the whole his poems show no great literary merit. But he was known and remembered as a saint, and two of his hymns, those for Morning and Evening Prayer, have passed into the common use of English-speaking Christians throughout the world.

What concerns us here, however, are his Marian poems, of which there are a number. They provide a late but interesting example of the characteristic Anglican piety of their time. While the great majority of these poems, together with Ken's other devotional writings, have fallen into oblivion, four stanzas have passed into fairly common liturgical use among Anglicans through their incorporation into one of the standard English hymnbooks, and have thus become part of our liturgical heritage.

Her virgin eyes saw God incarnate born
When she to Bethle'em came that happy morn
How high her raptures then began to swell
Non but her own omniscient Son can tell.

As Eve when she her fontal sin reviewed
Wept for herself and all she should include,
Blest Mary, with man's Saviour in embrace
Joyed for herself and for all human race.

All saints are by her Son's dear influence bless'd
She kept the very fountain at her breast,
The Son adored and nursed by the sweet Maid
A thousandfold of love for love repaid.

Heaven with transcendent joys her entrance graced
Next to his throne, her Son his mother placed
And here below, now she's of heaven possess'd
All generations are to call her bless'd.[1]

Seen against the background of the writings of Taylor and Frank, Ken's position in this hymn seems in no way eccentric. We find in his lines themes with which we have already become familiar. In particular we see in them the contrast of Eve with Mary, a comparison first made in the second century of the Christian era. The affirmation of faith in the assumption implied in the final stanza, is perhaps more explicit than it would have been in most of Ken's contemporaries. But it is not exceptional.

The eighteenth century was not a time in which Marian devotion might be expected to flourish in the Church of England. In hymnody the doctrine of the incarnation itself found magnificent expression in the Christmas hymns of Charles Wesley.

> Let heaven and earth combine,
> Angels and men agree
> To praise in hymns divine,
> The incarnate deity,
> Our God contracted to a span
> Incomprehensibly made man.[2]

A similar classical expression of this doctrine is to be found in the poetry of Christopher Smart.

> God all-bounteous, all-creative
> Whom no ills from good dissuade
> Is incarnate and a native
> Of the very world he made.[3]

And in Christopher Smart there is also a magnificent expression of the faith that everything in creation has its part in praising God. But neither poet seems to have been led to meditate at any length on the figure of Mary, and the verses in which Charles Wesley does refer to her attracted the disapproval of his brother.

With the beginnings of the romantic movement, however, a feeling for the place of Mary in the Christian scheme of things begins to revive. There are many reasons for this. In part it was due to a revolution in attitudes towards the Middle Ages. Suddenly much that seemed admirable and attractive was discovered in the faith and devotion of centuries which had previously been regarded as simply barbarous. In part it was due to a new respect for woman, and a new interest in the feminine element in human experience. It was also, we may suspect, linked with a new feeling for the unity of humankind with nature. Certainly all these factors were at work in the poetry of William Wordsworth and had their part in producing his remarkable sonnet to our Lady, in which she is addressed as 'our tainted nature's solitary boast'.

Within the Church of England as a whole these tendencies did not have their full effect until after the coming of the Oxford Movement in the 1830s. But already in the first part of the nineteenth century their influence was being felt, not least in the work of a man like Bishop Reginald Heber, missionary, evangelist and hymn-writer. It is interesting to place his hymn about Mary, written explicitly for use in the liturgy, next to the lines of Thomas Ken which we have already quoted. Between them they might be taken to sum up the whole tradition of pre-Tractarian Anglican devotion to Mary. Indeed in the admirable balance with which Heber holds together the Lord to whom the hymn is addressed with the mother whose blessedness it celebrates, we might see something which could be taken as representative of the Anglican tradition as a whole.

Virgin-born, we bow before thee,
Blessed was the womb that bore thee,
Mary, mother meek and mild
Blessed was she in her child.

Blessed was the breast that fed thee,
Blessed was the hand that led thee,
Blessed was the parent's eye
That watched thy slumbering infancy.

Blessed she by all creation,
Who brought forth the world's salvation,
And blessed they, for ever blest
Who love thee most and serve thee best.

Virgin-born we bow before thee,
Blessed was the womb that bore thee,
Mary, mother meek and mild,
Blessed was she in her child.[4]

There is something remarkable about this hymn which for all its apparent simplicity manages to say so much in so small a space. Who was its author, and how does he come to have such insight?

Heber was a man who might indeed be called a representative Anglican, if such a being really exists. He was closely associated with the Evangelicals of his day, at that time by far the most dynamic element within the Church. Yet he dissociated himself from the Calvinism of their theology, and explicitly accepted the name of an Arminian. Like others of his contemporaries he turned his attention to the writings of the seventeenth-century divines. In Heber's case this interest led him to produce an edition of the works of Jeremy Taylor, prefaced by a biography. It is interesting to see some of the qualities in Taylor which Heber particularly admired. He commends 'the wise, and moderate, and eminently Christian spirit of Jeremy Taylor . . . his zeal for the essentials of the Catholic faith; his abhorrence of unprofitable and vexatious grounds of difference; his piety, his toleration and his humility'.[5] His discussion of *The Great Exemplar*, Taylor's Life of Christ, is no less interesting. While he expresses some surprise at its lack of any critical and historical sense, (the work, he tells us, 'relates with almost the same apparent faith, the salutation of the angel to the Virgin Mary; the Syriac prayer attributed to Christ at his baptism by St Philoxenus; and the prostration of the Egyptian idols when the infant Jesus came into their country'), he shows no sign of being disturbed by the exuberance of the Marian passages which we have quoted, and which certainly were not typical of the piety of his own time.

Like the great majority of Anglicans before the Oxford Movement, Heber was fiercely anti-Roman. Although in traditional Anglican fashion he has no hesitation in speaking of the Catholic faith and of the Catholic Church, to which his own Church belongs, he has no doubt that he is a Protestant. But here again we must not assume too readily that we know all that this term implies. It is easy to read back into the past, attitudes which do not belong there. In Heber's case his Protestantism goes with a very high doctrine of episcopacy. When at the age of forty he accepted to go to India as the second bishop of Calcutta, he found himself exercising an episcopal ministry far outside the bounds of the established Church. In these circumstances he did not hesitate to appeal to the apostolic authority of his office.

A bishop, as such, is not the creature of the civil magistrate. His authority existed before the civil power had recognised him; it existed while the civil sword was bared against him, in its fullest cruelty; it is recognised as existing already and independently of the civil power, in those very enactments whereby the civil power controls and regulates its exercise. And whether it is found in a state of depression and discountenance, as in the episcopal Church of Scotland, or in a state of persecution, as in the episcopal Church of Greece, or altogether unconnected with the civil institutions of the land, as in the episcopal Churches of North America and Malayalim, it admits no other, and it can seek no nobler source of its authority than that of 'as my Father hath sent me, so send I you. . .'[6]

Here, in this remarkable panorama of episcopal Christendom, which takes in Anglican Churches in Scotland and North America, Syrian Churches in South India, and the Orthodox Church of Greece, we find the convictions of the Oxford Movement about the apostolic character of the bishop's office, clearly stated more than a decade before John Keble preached his Assize sermon. Doubtless in Heber's mind the doctrine did not have the full theological weight which it would acquire for the Tractarians, with their vision of the episcopate as the keystone of the whole sacramental structure of the Church. It is there nonetheless, firm and uncompromising. Heber was prepared to act on these convictions in his dealings with his own clergy, and in his relations with the bishops both of the Syrian Church in South India, and of the Armenian communities in the north of the sub-continent. He had particularly close contact with the latter, inviting their clergy to take part in his ordinations, and receiving one of their deacons as a student at Bishop's College, Calcutta.

That the Oxford Movement would change much in the shape of the Anglican tradition is unquestionable. One of the places where we can see this very clearly is in a change of attitude towards other Churches, and in particular towards Rome. If Heber sought contacts with the Oriental Churches it was in order that they should reform themselves after the Anglican model, rather than the other way about. Less than a generation later, young men would be travelling to France from Oxford and Cambridge in order to discover how to reform the Church of England according to the model which they saw there. The criterion of Christian excellence was for them no longer to be found solely or even principally within the Church of England. Between 1823 and 1845 much would have altered in Anglicanism in a way which could not be reversed. There was a new enthusiasm, not only for the early centuries and the Middle Ages, but also for much of contemporary Roman Catholicism. In all these different places, Marian devotion was to be found.

But the passages which we have quoted from Heber suggest that not all was innovation. The commonly held view that the Oxford Movement marks a complete break in Anglican tradition, whether for good or ill, needs to be revised. More often than not it was giving new expression to old convictions, which had been in part forgotten or obscured. Its insistence on the apostolic authority of the episcopate, its feeling of kinship with the ancient Churches of the Christian East, its desire to affirm a degree of reverence for the Mother of the Lord, these were all things which the new movement shared with high-churchmen of an earlier generation. Reginald Heber's hymns express that earlier tradition very well and show that it has a substance which we should not underestimate. It is in different areas that we should look for what is most characteristic of the life and message of the Oxford leaders, in a new attitude to the Catholic Church of the West, a new apprehension of the consequences to be drawn from the doctrine of the incarnation, and a new sense of the sacramental character of all creation. It is to these points that we shall be turning in the next chapter.

NOTES
1 *English Hymnal*, no. 217
2 *Methodist Hymn Book*, no. 142
3 Christopher Smart, 'The Nativity of Our Lord', *Poets of the English Language*, ed. W. H. Auden and N. H. Pearson, vol. iii (London 1952), p. 554

4   *English Hymnal*, no. 640
5   *The Works of Jeremy Taylor*, ed. Reginald Heber (Oxford 1821), p. viii
6   *The Life of Reginald Heber*, DD, by his widow (1830), vol. ii, p. 163

6

John Keble and the Oxford Movement

The theology of the Oxford Movement, though it has often enough been described, has not yet been sufficiently studied in depth. What was it that gave to the movement such vitality and strength, intellectual, spiritual and practical alike? We have already suggested that however important the questions of the apostolic authority of the ministry and of the Church's fundamental independence of the state may have been, there were other concerns which lay nearer to the heart of the movement. Of these, without question, the most significant was the renewed sense of the meaning and consequences of the doctrine of the incarnation. At the centre of their prayer and life, the leaders of the movement affirmed their faith in the nearness of God, of God who approaches men everywhere and in everything, yet who has committed himself absolutely to the flesh and blood of his Church, which is the very Body of Christ. It was this faith which filled them alike with awe and rejoicing, giving them both an awareness of the sacramental nature of all creation, and a sense of the particular fleshly nature of the sacrament of all sacraments, Christ the incarnate Lord.

In the brief but highly perceptive introduction to his selection of Tractarian texts, *The Oxford Movement*, Dr Eugene Fairweather writes: 'The Tractarians saw the Incarnation, the Church and the sacraments as contiguous and inseparable elements in God's redemptive economy. For the Tractarians, as for all orthodox Christians, the heart of Christianity was the story of God's own saving and self-revealing action, which culminated in the hypostatic union of humanity with deity in the person of the mediator. But they did not stop here. To their minds it was no less clearly a part of the Christian message that the saving person and work of the Mediator were effectually "represented" in the Church by means of certain sacramental "extensions of the Incarnation". It was, they insisted, supremely fitting that the life-giving flesh and blood of God's Eternal Son who was made man should be communicated through fleshly signs wrought by human hands. Indeed they were prepared to argue that failure to recognize the "extensions of the Incarnation" stemmed from a feeble apprehension of the twofold truth of the Incarnation itself – on the one hand, that man's salvation comes from God alone; on the other, that God's saving action really penetrates and transforms man's world and man's life.'[1]

On the one hand the Reformation insistence on the priority of God's action was maintained; on the other the materiality of that action in the sacraments, 'transforming man's world and man's life' was asserted in a way which seemed shocking to the religious mind of the England of that day. Pusey in his lectures on 'Types and Prophecies', given in 1836, and, though never published, a primary source for understanding the theology of the movement in its formative stages, writes:

> The whole system of religion, contemplative and practical, is one of God's condescension; God cometh down to us, not we mount up to God. Its corner-stone and characteristic is 'God manifest in the flesh', and with this, as God has appointed it, all is in keeping. Neither the letter without the Spirit, nor yet the Spirit without the letter – prayers, which God cometh into the midst of us to hear; earthly Sacraments, yet full of Heaven; earthly words yet full of the Word, *Logoi*, proceeding from and setting forth the *Logos*.[2]

Here already we see many of the themes of the seventeenth-century theologians coming into view again, in particular that sense of the redemption of the body, in which it will be natural to speak about the place of Mary in the whole scheme of man's salvation.

In seeking to reaffirm the coinherence of man and nature, to see the natural world no less than man's personal experience as the field of the divine activity, the Tractarians were of course involved in very great difficulties. The intellectual atmosphere of their time hardly supported them in their endeavour. However, they were able to find at least some allies. They were deeply aware of their indebtedness to Wordsworth, with his vision of the sacramental character of the natural world; both Keble and Pusey speak of this explicitly. Partly through his assistance, it was possible to see the sacraments of the Church not in isolation but set against the background of a universe, sacramental at every point. There were theological implications in his writing which Wordsworth himself had hardly seen. There was also the pervasive if ill-defined influence of Coleridge whose ideas were 'in the air', so that even those who had not read him seem unable to have wholly escaped their influence.[3]

In his lectures on 'Types and Prophecies', Pusey attempts to see the typical and prophetic character of the Scriptures not only in relation to the sacramental order of the Church, but also in relation to a sacramental understanding of the universe as a whole, and to the whole of human history. He quotes Hooker, whose writings had suddenly become relevant and alive again; all things are partakers of God in that 'God hath his influences into the very essence of all things, without which influence of Deity supporting them their utter annihilation could not choose but follow'. He goes on to refer to Wordsworth and Keble as writers whose works exhibit the power of God at work in nature, and he quotes four curiously undistinguished lines from 'The Christian Year' which seem to have been adopted by the Tractarians (Newman also quotes them) as a kind of slogan to express their conviction that to those with eyes to see, everything proclaims the glory of God.

Every leaf in every nook
Every wave in every brook
Chanting with a solemn voice
Mind us of our better choice.

But not only this; he further suggests that while the sacred history of the Old Testament points explicitly towards Christ, there is at least an implicit acknowledgement of him throughout the whole of human history.

This inherent significance of images receives its full direction and completeness in God's revelation. In heathenism and in the natural world they are significant but not of necessity prophetic. They express truth, but give no earnest that it shall be realized, unless indeed in so far as we may

See in heaven and earth
In all fair things around
Strong yearnings for a blest new birth
With sinless glories crowned,

and in some way the very existence of imperfect good does prophesy of its completion somewhere. Thus the heathen history is instructive, not prophetic, or prophetic in a general way and in broad outlines, of the course of that natural providence of God whereof it testifies and whereby it was produced.

The seventeenth-century attempts to see all things in the light of God's activity in creation and redemption is taken up and reaffirmed in a new and less congenial climate. In the theology of the early Tractarians there was to be no retreat from the external world into an inner world of piety alone. Man is an enfleshed being, and the whole manner of God's activity demands that inner and outer concur in one. The sacramental principle which extends to the whole creation, demands no less than this. All is centred in one focal point, the incarnation of the Word of God; yet this mysterious act flows out and has its effects everywhere. Furthermore the divine grace which descends into the world does so in order that the whole creation may be lifted up, made new, brought into the Kingdom of heaven. Man is to be raised up into communion of life with God, a restoration of unity which will be no less than the marriage of heaven and earth.

In a note on a poem on the marriage at Cana in Galilee, Keble writes:

The change of water into wine was believed by the ancients to typify the change which St Paul in particular so earnestly dwells on: 'Old things are become new.' And St John, 'He that sitteth on the Throne saith, Behold I make all things new.' Accordingly St Cyprian applies the first miracle to the admission of the Gentiles into the Church (Ep. 63, ed. Fell). And St Augustine to the

Evangelical interpretation of the Old Testament (in John, Tract 8). And St Cyril of Alexandria (in Cor.) to the Spirit superseding the letter. This then being the beginning of miracles, a kind of pattern of the rest, showed how Christ's glory was to be revealed in the effects of His Sacramental Touch; whether immediately, as when He touched the leper and healed him, or through the hem of His garment, or by the Saints, His living members according to His Promise, 'the works that I do ye shall do also; and greater works than these shall ye do, because I go unto My Father.' Thus according to the Scriptures, the Sacramental Touch of the Church is the Touch of Christ, and her system is 'deifica disciplina', a rule which, in some sense, makes men gods, and the human divine; and all this depends on the verity of the Incarnation, therefore His Mother is especially instrumental in it; besides being, as nearest to Him, the most glorious instance of it. 'The Mother of Jesus is there, and both Jesus and His disciples are called.' (He as the Bridegroom and Author of the whole mystery, they as ministers, servants and instruments) – to this mysterious 'marriage' or Communion of Saints.[4]

In this vision of the faith, Mary's position has again become central. Not that she is herself the author of salvation, but the one in whom and through whom we come to know the mystery of the Word made flesh. Not herself, as Mark Frank would say, the object of man's worship, but the place where that object is to be found; 'especially instrumental' in the work of man's salvation. And because that instrumentality is in no way mechanical or automatic, but entirely dependent on her own free and personal decision, she is as nearest to him, the most glorious instance of that work of restoration, the first of saints, the Queen of heaven. Furthermore, in this vision of things as Keble expounds it, the doctrine of our deification by God's grace, clearly present in the seventeenth century, but more and more obscured in the following period, has made its reappearance. For it is only in the context of this doctrine that the whole development of devotion to Mary can make sense. Isolated from this setting, the extravagant praises which the tradition has loved to heap upon her become unbalanced indeed and verge on idolatry. Here in this reaffirmation of the fullness of the doctrine of the incarnation, so wonderfully expressed in what is simply an explanatory note to a poem, we find the root of the whole subsequent development of devotion to Mary within that particular tradition which stems from the things which took place in Oxford in the ten or so years following on 1833.

There was, however, another way in which the figure of Mary acquired a central importance for the Tractarians; through their very specific attitude towards childhood. That there can be something sentimental in this it would be difficult to deny. But it would be still more unperceptive not to see that there is in it something more than sentiment. If the Tractarians devoted a great part of their time to church history, it was not simply because they were antiquarians (though some of them were). Rather they believed that origins were important, for societies and individuals alike, that the past was not something left behind, but that in the communion of saints the past was gathered up so as to be a living reality in the present. In the history of the people of God, in the working out of the mystery of the incarnation itself, time allows for the unfolding of a gift which was already there in principle, given in the beginning.

What was true of the whole people of God was, they believed, true of the life of each one. 'The child is father of the man.' Here again we find a typically romantic interest in the pre-conscious, pre-rational areas of human life and experience. So in his lectures on 'Types and Prophecies', in refuting the dry eighteenth-century way of using the Old Testament texts as so many simple predictions of future events, Pusey says:

What then appears to me of primary importance as a corrective of this narrow view of prophecy is to have well impressed on the mind the significant character of everything which comes from God. The world is full of types and it were probably true to say everything is a type if we could realize it. The words of a child are constantly typical of the future developed being; they speak greater truth than they themselves (the outward organ of truth) know: they speak it in reference to some particular occasion, but indefinitely; they are aware of something kindred to the whole truth, and have some glimmering of it, but it they cannot grasp. And yet they who hear it will rightly wonder at it, and they who understand it better than the child itself, will yet confess that they could not have uttered it so simply and so forcibly. Its very indefiniteness adds to its reality, comprehensiveness, energy. It comes not from the child itself, but from a power within it; they are in truth the words of God, in the mouth of the little one, so lately come from its Maker's hand. In like manner, the sayings of the Old Testament, tho' they often have not the distinct outline of truth, which belongs to the development, have in them continually a depth of shade, which impresses the mind in the midst of its indistinctiveness, yet more forcibly, and has more religious awe than would the mere outline, tho' ever so distinct.

The Wordsworthian echoes in this passage are too evident to need comment.

What is said here of the Old Testament could also be applied in some measure to the writings of the Fathers, as contrasted with the strictness of definition which comes in medieval scholasticism. Pusey himself makes the comparison later in these lectures. Clarity is not all. Images speak more powerfully and with greater 'awe' than concepts, however distinct. In speaking of divine realities, images which can be interpreted at many levels and which do not attempt to say everything, are frequently less inadequate than concepts, which can deceive by their very clarity, giving us a feeling of having mastered and comprehended things which we can only truly understand if we are prepared ourselves to be mastered and comprehended by them. In this preference for original statements of truth in all the fullness and indefiniteness of their meaning, we are surely not wrong in seeing at least an indirect influence of Coleridge. Thomas MacFarland, in his immensely erudite study of the religious element in Coleridge's thought, deals at some length with the importance for Coleridge of transcending a purely linear view of growth. He comments: 'We too often think of "development" as a kind of progress up a series of steps, the improvement of one's position by the abandonment of a previous position. Actually the word implies an unwrapping of something already there. Its sister words in German and French suggest the same psychological truth; *Entwicklung* implies an unwrapping, *épanouissement*, a flowering from a bud. . . Though the data of the world change for us, and their connexions with our understanding, the eyes looking out from our time-eroded bodies are the lights of a soul that does not change.'[5] In this way of understanding how the past is recapitulated in the present, to which reference was made at the very beginning of this book, the Tractarians would have found something which touched them very nearly, a principle vital for their understanding both of human personality and of church tradition, a way of seeing how through time, time may be transcended into eternity.

We begin now to be aware of some of the factors which lay behind the Tractarian interest in childhood. We are less surprised to find that Keble's second volume of hymns and poems, *Lyra Innocentium*, is composed of meditations on the words and actions of children. We begin to see too why it was natural that the thought of the childhood of Jesus and his relationship to his mother was one which came easily to Keble's mind. *Lyra Innocentium* appeared in 1846, the year after Newman's conversion, and the numerous references to Mary in the book caused some anxiety to Keble's friends. How much greater their anxiety would have been had they known that the most deeply felt of all the Marian poems written for it had been excluded from the collection at the insistence of some of Keble's closest friends, who feared that, at that moment, it would lead to unwelcome controversy. Only later in his life did Keble publish this remarkable piece, 'Mother out of Sight'.

The poem, which is dated to the autumn of 1844, takes its origin from a seemingly trivial incident, involving a small boy, who comes rushing into the room expecting to greet his mother, only to find to his intense disappointment that 'Mother is not here'. The time at which the poem is written is significant. Already by the end of 1844, the shadow of Newman's departure began to be seen. The bishops and the general public were showing themselves universally hostile. The high hopes which had characterized the previous decade, when all seemed to prosper for the Oxford Movement, suddenly looked very insubstantial. It is in this situation that Keble pens these lines of a passionate intensity, whose stress raises his verse on this occasion to a poetic level which it seldom reaches. Yes, he seems to say, Mary may be very little in evidence in the Church

of England; the Church herself may seem a cold and distant mother.
And yet still the Church is there, and still Mary is there at its heart,
the one who hears the Word of God and keeps it.

Mother of God! O not in vain
We learned of old thy lowly strain.
Fain in thy shadow would we rest
And kneel with thee, and call thee blest.
With thee would 'magnify the Lord',
And if thou art not here adored
Yet seek we, day by day, the love and fear
Which bring thee, with all Saints, near and more near.

What glory thou above hast now,
By special grace of thy dear Son,
We see not yet, nor dare espy
Thy crowned form with open eye.
Rather beside the manger meek
Thee bending with veiled brow we seek,
Or where the Angel in the thrice-great-Name
Hail'd thee and Jesus to thy bosom came.

Yearly since then with bitterer cry,
Man hath assail'd the Throne on high,
And sin and hate, more fiercely striven
To mar the league 'twixt earth and heaven.
But the dread tie, that pardoning hour,
Made fast in Mary's awful bower,
Hath mightier proved to bind than we to break.
None may that work undo, that Flesh unmake.

Henceforth, whom thousand worlds adore,
He calls thee Mother evermore;
Angel nor Saint His face may see
Apart from what He took of thee.
How may we choose but name thy name
Echoing below their high acclaim
In holy Creeds? Since earthly song and prayer
Must keep faint time to the dread anthem there.

How but in love on thine own days,
Thou blissful one, upon thee gaze?
Nay every day, each suppliant hour
Whenever we kneel in aisle or bower,
Thy glories we may greet unblamed
Nor shun the lay by seraphs framed,
'Hail Mary, full of grace!' O, welcome sweet,
Which daily in all lands all saints repeat!

Fair greeting, with our matin vows
Paid duly to the enthroned Spouse,
His Church and Bride, here and on high,
Figured in her deep purity,
Who, born of Eve, high mercy won,
To bear and nurse the Eternal Son.
O, awful station, to no seraph given,
On this side touching sin, on the other heaven!

Therefore as kneeling day by day,
We to our Father duteous pray.
So unforbidden may we speak
An Ave to Christ's Mother meek;
(As children with 'good morrow' come
To elders in some happy home);
Inviting so the saintly host above
With our unworthiness to pray in love.[6]

The poem, as often happens with Keble, is less easy to interpret than might appear at first sight, or rather, and perhaps purposely, it lends itself to a variety of interpretations. What exactly does the phrase, 'On this side touching sin, on the other heaven', mean? Is it a quiet repudiation of the doctrine of the immaculate conception, not at that time a *de fide* dogma of the Roman Catholic Church, or is it more general in its intent? Do the words, 'and if thou art not here adored', mean 'and though here you are properly not given the worship which is due to God, yet . . .' or 'and even though you are not given that adoring love which is your due, yet. . .'? Does the second verse cast doubt on the doctrine of the assumption, or does it merely say that we should concentrate our thought on Mary's role at Bethlehem? We do not intend here to try to answer these questions. Knowing how easy it is to misinterpret Keble's mind, much more subtly patterned than most commentators allow, (the classic example of misunderstanding occurred in Keble's own lifetime over the words declaring that the Lord gives himself in the Eucharist 'not in the hands but in the heart', words which were taken to imply a denial of the real presence, a thing which Keble made it clear he had never intended), we leave such detailed questions for a larger one concerning the whole movement of the stanzas in question.[7]

None of the leaders of the Oxford Movement was more consistently faithful to the post-Reformation tradition of the Church of England than Keble. 'What my father taught me' was his constant point of reference. For him the seventeenth-century tradition was not something to be laboriously unearthed from the past, it was something, which at least in principle, he knew as a living reality which he had received in his own childhood, in observing the faith and practice of the older John Keble. In the first of the stanzas quoted, Keble refers to having learnt from his earliest years, through the daily recitation of the Magnificat at Evensong, to pray with Mary and to be aware that she and all the saints were near. But in the fourth and fifth stanzas, he is saying something more than that. He is saying that we can and should contemplate the example of Mary not only on her own feast days, but every day; and that we should not be afraid to address her directly, using ourselves the words of the angel, 'Hail Mary, full of grace', a welcome which 'daily in all lands all saints repeat'.

Keble was well aware that, almost without exception, the seventeenth-century theologians had discountenanced any direct address to the Blessed Virgin or to the saints as liable to lead to dangerous consequences and especially to an equation of the creature with the Creator. To ask God to hear the prayers of the saints on our behalf, as is done in the Canon of the Roman Mass, is one thing, and some of the earlier Anglicans maintained – Richard Field and Herbert Thorndike, for instance – that it is not only permissible but admirable to do so. To ask the saints directly for their intercession is something else. George Herbert had written a poem explicitly on this question, in which he says that he would have gladly turned to Mary for assistance, had he had any warrant from the Lord for doing so. But not having such an authority, he dare not go beyond what Scripture seems to prescribe. And here is Keble asserting that this practice, which nearly all Anglicans since the Reformation had abandoned, is one which has the support of 'all saints in all lands'. He is being, in fact, almost as provocative as W. G. Ward, or those of Newman's younger and more enthusiastic disciples, who were asserting clearly that the norms of catholicity were not to be found in the Church of England at all, but elsewhere in Catholic Christendom.

What had happened to bring about this firm conviction in a man who did not commit himself to changes without careful thought? The factors involved become clear in the third of the stanzas quoted. There may be dangers in an exaggerated cult of Mary and the saints, but they are not very menacing for nineteenth-century Englishmen. On the other hand there are dangers which had already been seen in embryo in the seventeenth century – we recall Mark Frank speaking of 'our Lady being wounded through our Lady's side' – dangers which have now grown to monstrous proportions. There is the possibility of a complete rejection of the religion of the incarnation, a rejection which will sometimes be explicit and total, sometimes more gradual and insidious, beginning with a rejection of those doctrines and practices which, as we have seen, the Tractarians believed to be bound up inseparably with a right faith in God the Word's taking our human nature. In face of these dangers, it is only through an outspoken and explicit acknowledgement of Mary's part in the work of redemption, that we can hope to maintain the true proportions and the fullness of the faith. In face of a wholly changed situation, the reserve of the seventeenth-century Anglicanism no longer has the meaning it once had. It should be abandoned.

The Tractarians were not alone in the nineteenth century in being aware of these dangers and in making this kind of response. All over Europe the same signs could be seen. At least one outstanding voice in the Lutheran world was raised at this time in honour of Mary, in order to safeguard the central truth of the incarnation. This is not the place to cite at length the works of N. F. S. Grundtvig (1783–1872), the Danish churchman, educationalist, preacher and hymn writer, whose activity is so unjustly ignored in the English-speaking world. But certainly his hymns and poems contain material vital for any full understanding of the place of Mary in the faith and piety of continental Protestantism.

Gud os gav hans Søn til Broder
Jesus Christus Gud og man
Salig prise vi hans Moder
Himlens Brud i Jomfrustand.

God gave us his Son to be our Brother
Jesus Christ, God and Man
So we praise his blessed Mother
The Virgin Bride of heaven.

We may also suppose that it was considerations such as these which were among the factors which prompted the enormous growth of Marian theology and devotion in the Roman Catholic Church at this period. Some elements of this development, particularly its extreme elaboration and refinement of theological speculation, must seem to anyone looking at it from outside that particular tradition (and perhaps to some within it) to be unbalanced and aberrant. Others, such as the proclamation of the two Marian dogmas of 1854 and 1950, raise difficult questions for the relationship between separated Christians; though it would be the general thesis of this book, that they can only be treated fruitfully when placed in a larger and more inclusive context than has often been the case. But the most important, the most challenging and in some ways the most perplexing element in all this development, is one not often mentioned in ecumenical discussions, because not formally an obstacle to Christian unity. I refer to the appearances of our Lady in various places in Western Europe in the last 130 years, and quite specifically to the two main original apparitions in France, at La Salette (1846) and at Lourdes (1858). Here are events, mysterious indeed in the biblical as well as in the popular sense of that word; events which have influenced and which do influence the lives of millions of people and have become part of the history of Western Catholicism. It is not difficult to raise critical and sceptical questions about both events. It is more difficult for someone who is not living within the direct stream of faith and piety in which they occurred, to assess them positively. What was God doing there? What is God doing now in these places? Are we dealing with a deep and perhaps vitally important stirring within the Christian consciousness? Or is it perhaps both these things? The fact that in both cases the ones who saw were children and ill educated should only increase our respect for the mysteriousness of what occurred. Something was given at La Salette and Lourdes. Whatever it was, Mélanie and her companions at La Salette, Bernadette at Lourdes did not manufacture it.

At the time when Keble was writing his hymn, none of these events had taken place. The whole climate of opinion in nineteenth-century England hardly allowed Anglicans as a whole to take them seriously when they did. There were exceptions, however, and one at least we would wish to know more about. In 1865 B. F. Westcott went to La Salette and was so much interested by what he saw there that when he came home he wrote a report on his visit. Once again friends intervened to prevent an imprudent publication. The matter was too dangerous. The report was never published, but only privately printed and circulated. We can hardly suppose that Westcott was wholly uncritical of what he saw. But evidently he was also deeply impressed. No one would have suggested his suppressing a simple denunciation of peasant superstition. That would have been entirely acceptable in nineteenth-century England. Perhaps now when the atmosphere of confidence and understanding between separated Christians is so much stronger than it was, it is time to look at these and kindred subjects together in a new way.[8]

Meanwhile it is clear that a renewal of devotion to Mary, indeed a new development of that devotion, is something which comes from the very heart of the faith and prayer of the Oxford Movement. It is in John Keble himself, in Newman's judgement 'the true and original author' of the whole movement, that we can see this most distinctly. If in subsequent developments of Anglo-Catholicism, elements of counter-Reformation devotion were sometimes borrowed uncritically and even artificially, the roots of this recovery of the Church's traditional attitude towards the Mother of the Lord are to be found at the heart of the concerns

114

of the first leaders of this movement which began in the university of Oxford in the decade following 1833.

NOTES
1 *The Oxford Movement*, ed. E. R. Fairweather, p. 11
2 For a fuller account of these lectures, the ms. of which is at Pusey House, Oxford, see my article 'The Theological Vision of the Oxford Movement', in *The Rediscovery of Newman*, ed. John Coulson and A. M. Allchin (1966)
3 On this subject see Stephen Prickett's two admirable books, *Coleridge and Wordsworth, The Poetry of Growth* (Cambridge 1970) and *Romanticism and Religion, The Tradition of Coleridge and Wordsworth in the Victorian Church* (Cambridge 1976)
4 Quoted in *The Rediscovery of Newman*
5 T. Macfarland, *Coleridge and the Pantheist Tradition* (Oxford 1969), pp. 161–2
6 John Keble, *Miscellaneous Poems* (Oxford 1870), pp. 256–9
7 Even so perceptive and authoritative a historian as Owen Chadwick shares the widely held underestimation of Keble's original and subtle mind. Cf. the introduction to his anthology *The Mind of the Oxford Movement* (1960)
8 Arthur Westcott, *The Life and Letters of Brooke Foss Westcott*, 2 vols. (London 1903) vol. i, pp. 245–6

Part Three

Voices of the Twentieth Century

7

'The Ferment of Birth': Euros Bowen

All the writers whose work we have examined so far have belonged to the Anglican tradition. Euros Bowen, to whom we now turn, is no exception to this. As a priest of the Church in Wales, an autonomous province of the Anglican Communion, he stands within the same tradition of prayer and faith as Lancelot Andrewes or John Keble. But as a poet, who handles with consummate skill the literary methods and techniques of classical Welsh verse, he brings to his writing another and older heritage than that of the English. It is too often forgotten that the island of Britain contains not one but two living literary languages, and that the senior of them is Welsh. Despite the fact that the very existence of the language is today in peril, the poetic achievement of twentieth-century Wales – the century of Saunders Lewis and Gwenallt Jones, to mention only two outstanding names – can stand comparison with the earlier centuries of this rich and extraordinarily persistent literary tradition. Moreover, the fact that in Welsh-speaking Wales the poet's craft is still a common pursuit and a common interest, gives to the writer in Welsh a public position and relevance which his English-speaking counterpart does not have. As in Russia, for instance, the poet knows that what he says can be of meaning and importance to a great variety of people. His words will be quoted in a political trial, for instance.

It is not only the literary and social position of the Welsh writer which differs from that of the English. His religious heritage is also in some ways significantly different. The history of the Welsh people in the last two centuries has been influenced by the Methodist revival, which began in the first part of the eighteenth century, to a degree which has no parallel in England. The strict Calvinism of the Welsh Methodist movement, in this respect somewhat different from Wesleyan Methodism, and the rejection of the arts which often went with it, have led in our century to a strong reaction. While in some writers this has expressed itself in a desire to reassert pre-Christian cultural values, in others there has been a renewed apprehension of the sacramental character of the Christian vision. One of the striking things about this Christian poetry of twentieth-century Wales is that its writers have belonged to different denominations. Saunders Lewis, himself the outstanding figure in Welsh letters in our time, has become a Roman Catholic. Gwenallt embraced for some years an Anglican Catholicism. Waldo Williams, originally a Baptist, entered the Society of Friends. But all have sought to see God not over against, but in and through, the gifts which he is giving us. In place of the world-rejecting attitudes of Calvinistic Methodism, it has been the purpose of these writers to see the whole world shot through with the divine glory, to find sacraments of the presence of the Lord who took flesh, in the very substance of the world around them.

In many ways Euros Bowen has his place within this group. Coming from a Congregational background, he was confirmed into the Church in Wales during his years as a student, accepting what he himself terms the tradition of classical Christianity. Certainly his whole understanding of the Christian faith and of the world is sacramental through and through. His poetic style, however, has developed in ways which have no exact parallels among his contemporaries. For, as well as being a master of the classical forms, he has shown himself a brilliant innovator in poetic techniques. To literary critics in Wales, his work has suggested a comparison with the great symbolist poets, French and Russian, of the earlier part of this century.

Bowen himself, however, prefers to describe his poetic method as sacramental rather than symbolist. For him it is of vital significance that the sacramental retains its earthly substance. The symbol is not dissolved in the thing symbolized. The bread of the Eucharist signifies and indeed *is* more than bread. But it is in and through

120

the bread that this 'more' becomes present. Everything in this world can become an image, a sacrament of something greater than itself. It is the poet's task to perceive this. But in doing so, the particularity, the specific nature of the created is not destroyed. The theological principle articulated by Lancelot Andrewes is verified in the experience of the poet.

The use of imagery in the poems is thus not thought of by the poet simply as a play of the creative imagination. Rather it is seen as rooted in the very nature of things, in a world which is a world of sacraments and images, where the activity of God is at every stage sacramental. The heart and centre of this sacramental universe is to be found in the incarnation of the Word of God, and the image language of the poet is itself rooted in the image language of the Bible and the Church's liturgy. This language has its own particular structure or logic very different from that of abstract reasoning. At the end of a striking poem on the sacramental Word, the poet asserts that it is precisely through the enactment of the Church's central rite, the breaking of bread, that the word of grace is saved from becoming 'an ideology about Christ', a mere set of ideas and concepts about a long-dead master, rather than the living representation of his personal presence.

In such a vision of things, it is hardly surprising that the figure of Mary begins to find a place. It is, one might say, a general feature of Welsh writing that it refers rather readily to the figure of Mary and the saints. We may find striking references to our Lady in the writing both of Saunders Lewis and of Gwenallt, for example. More surprisingly, the Baptist New Testament scholar, John Gwili Jenkins, has a poem addressed to Mary in which he asks her pardon if she has been honoured less than God desires. But nowhere do we find so rich a treatment of the Mother of the Lord as in the ode by Euros Bowen called 'Genesis'. It is a treatment which both in its substance and its style has a majesty which demands our attention. As we shall see, the figure of Mary has a vital part to play in the whole pattern of the poem. The subject of the poem, which was entered for the National Eisteddfod of 1963, was suggested to the poet by a visit to the new Coventry Cathedral during the summer of the previous year. It is a meditation on the great window, with its abstract design, which is placed behind the font at the west end of the nave of the Church. As H. A. Hodges remarks, 'The writer was struck by the blaze of colour in the window itself, and by the splashes of colour which it throws upon walls and pillars, the polished floor and the unhewn stone of the font. All this is a "ferment" of colour, as he puts it, changing continually as the spectator changes his position, as the sun lowers in the sky and the atmospheric condition changes.' Euros Bowen himself says, 'I saw the window, the central light, the colours all round it and the whole baptistery in a ferment of Genesis. And that is the subject of the ode – the ferment of Genesis in and through the great window at Coventry . . . the genesis of the world, the genesis of Christ, the genesis of the Christian.'[1]

The writer tells us that this being a classical Christian theme, a classical poetic treatment seemed appropriate. This presents problems for the English reader. It is more than usually impossible to convey in translation the quality of the ancient Welsh poetic metres, established already in the early Middle Ages. The lines are full of *cynghanedd*, a device involving assonance, alliteration and internal rhymes. A single rhyme runs throughout the eighty lines of the first canto, and another through most of the lines of the third canto. But this does not concern us here. What is to the point for our purpose is the fact that the theology underlying the poem proves in its own way to be no less classical and precise than its form. It is a theology which has surprising affinities with that of the Eastern Christian tradition.

There is throughout the poem an astonishing wealth of constantly changing imagery in a 'ferment' of creation. The poet sees the divine activity of creation in and through the creation of the window. The shifting colours and shapes of the glass become an image of the varied aspects of the changing world of time through which the light of eternity shines. It is a poem full of images of fruitfulness, of peace, of brightness. The movement is slow and majestic, yet full of exuberance and a feeling of growth, for the ferment in the window creates a ferment in the poet's mind.

It is clear that it is the second canto, which speaks of the 'genesis' of Christ, which will most directly concern us. Yet it would be the greatest mistake to isolate it from what goes before and what follows after. The whole poem is a hymn of praise to the activity, the 'ferment' of the Spirit of God, of the uncreated, fruitful light of God, at work alike in creation, in incarnation, and in the birth of the Christian community. The three cantos of the poem, though quite distinct, are linked in a single movement. They form part of one whole.

The first canto celebrates the days of the creation. It reaches a climax in the stanza which tells of the creation of men. In the preceding lines the poet speaks of 'a silence whose peace held a ferment of morning', as it were a pause which ushers in the appearance of Adam. He proceeds: 'There in the church on a screen of gladness/I saw an acre between green trees,/ And a man there, set apart, royal, blessed,/His hands and their rule in the image of the Desire'.

There are many things to notice in these lines. First it is said explicitly that this takes place 'in the church' (*yn y llan*). (There is only one other place in the poem where these precise words occur.) At the literal level of meaning this refers only to the fact that the 'screen of gladness', the great many-hued window, is part of the church building. But it is surely not difficult to see a further reference to the vision which is to follow, the vision of man in Eden, in the church of paradise. This is particularly the case because the word *llan*, before it means church, means enclosure, a place set apart. Man is seen in his royal and priestly dignity, entering into creation as a king and a priest, having rule over the animals and the material order, living and working 'in the image of the Desire', (*ar ddelw'r Awydd.*) In this last phrase we have an interesting example of the theological precision of the writer. In the notes appended to the poem, he speaks of man as created (*ar ddelw Duw, ar lun Awydd y Crewr*) 'in the image of God, in the likeness of the Desire of the Creator'. It seems here that there is a reminiscence, conscious or not, of the patristic distinction between the image and the likeness of God, in man; the image, as it were the static, given character of God impressed upon his creature, the likeness the dynamic aspect, the character which is in becoming, which is to be worked out as man with his hands becomes a ruler and creator with God. The poet himself comments (in a private letter), 'I think of man as endowed on the finite level with creative freedom, God as creative freedom on the infinite level. *Awydd* implies the exercise of freedom.'

This word *awydd* (it is connected etymologically with *avidus*) may also give us pause. It might seem more obvious to speak of God as love, *agape, cariad*. But here are in fact many precedents in the Greek Fathers for speaking of *eros*, the desire of God, which calls out the answering desire in man. This is particularly the case in the writings of the fifth-century Syrian writer known as Dionysius the Areopagite, who, in view of the New Testament's constant use of *agape* to speak of the love of God, says somewhat paradoxically that *eros* is more divine than *agape*. The writings of Dionysius, however, have been immensely influential in Christian tradition, and there is something in his vision of the divine activity which can illuminate our understanding of the act of creation as it is celebrated in this poem. 'We must dare to add this as being no less true,' he writes, 'that the Source of all things Himself, in His wonderful and good love for all things, through the excess of His loving goodness, is carried outside Himself, in His providential care for all that is, so enchanted is He in goodness and love and longing. Removed from his position above all and beyond all He descends to be in all according to an ecstatic and transcendental power which is yet inseparable from Himself.'[2] This is a love which is ecstatic in the strict sense of that word, which carries God out from himself into creation, to dwell within the heart of things, so that he who is wholly transcendent becomes wholly present within his creation.

The next two stanzas speak of man in his innocence. 'His hope is a summer'; from the earth which he loves 'blameless hours' are his. He knows the light of birth, 'in increasing goodness/In peace and unction: he knows no shame'. In this first canto the fall is not spoken of.

The second canto of the poem is headed with the words 'he came down from heaven and took flesh by the Holy Ghost of the Virgin Mary'. In its course, the image of the garden which has been prepared in the previous lines blossoms out into a whole harvest of imagery of flower and plant. But the poet begins on a note of greater urgency, speaking of 'a ferment of birth, a white-hot ferment/Of fragile colours between strong pillars above the play of the ages'. Here as throughout the poem the primary reference is to the window itself, to the delicate patterning of its colours around the central sunburst, and the massive framework of its stone structure. The cathedral with its great window stands in the midst of the city 'like an ancient peace above the din of the city'. The city's life is itself in ferment, but it is only in the peace of the church that we begin to get glimpses of the pattern which gives meaning to that ferment, which is present within it yet often unperceived or not understood. The movements of human history are seen as a ferment of birth, a continuing genesis. The words *berw y geni*, ferment of birth, at once suggest an association between the Greek *genesis* and the Welsh *geni* (to be born) and its derivatives such as *genedigaeth* (birth). And suddenly in the midst of the ferment a form is discerned, 'like the brightest of flowers . . . a gentle virgin, like a heaven of snow'. The first meaning of the image of snow here is that of whiteness and purity. But maybe in the startling juxtaposition of images of winter and summer we may see a suggestion of the way in which the opposites come together when eternity touches time.

There follows a stanza in which a diversity of places and scenes are invoked to suggest the beauty of the Mother of Christ. 'The robe on the fair one of the bright childbearing/Is like quiet weather on Towyn's shore,/Like incense, again, from Dyfed itself,/An evening of splendour on Ynys Lochlyn,/Fair swirling waters at Aberglaslyn,/Bilberries trailing their myrrh on the Berwyns.' Two of the lines (2 and 4) speak of the golden beauty of the seashore at evening and in quiet weather. Two seem to hint at more distinctly ecclesiastical associations, the incense from Dyfed pointing to the shrine of St David, the reference to the myrrh on the Berwyns inescapably suggesting a reference to the great but humble hymn writer of the Berwyns, Ann Griffiths (1776–1805). Taken together the lines contain a discreet allusion to the gifts which the Magi brought to the infant Christ and his Mother, as a tribute from the nations of the world to the coming of the Messiah. All things are summoned to praise the beauty of the Creator revealed in the central beauty of the creature.

After a stanza which speaks of the moment of the annunciation, the poet, having summoned the images of nature, now summons the images of the scriptural tradition to clothe Mary: splendour of stars, a crescent moon, the cup of a lily, a rose of light. And in a very interesting way these images lead us forward into a second group of four stanzas, which speak of Mary less in herself, more as a figure of the Church. For the Church itself has its 'hours' of prayer and praise and silence, 'swiftly fly/The modes of their peace like a rich conversation'. At such moments of calm, the author comments in his own notes to the poem, 'the Holy Spirit as bridegroom of the soul comes to the garden, to the orchard, in a "respite which seems like a prophecy" of Mary'. All annunciations, all visitations of the Spirit in the Church come from and point to this central annunciation. And the poet does not only make use of images from Scripture. In the stanzas which follow he takes up the images of the Land of Rebirth and the Cauldron of Birth which occur in Celtic mythology. These too are fulfilled in this childbearing, and 'every province' of this land of new life is 'a homage to her'. In her all creation rejoices.

The final stanza of this group of four introduces a new and disturbing note to the imagery, a note which itself points towards what is to follow. We hear of 'the praise to the wine of the divine nature'. In his notes Bowen writes: 'In the orchard, in the vineyard in the church, the Virgin is a cup, a grail for the blood of the Spirit, "wedded to the praise of the Holy Spirit".' Despite the strangeness of speaking of the 'blood of the Spirit' (though St Paul in 1 Corinthians 12:13 speaks of our all drinking 'of one Spirit'), the language undoubtedly points to the cup of sacrifice, to the theme of redemption, which though it is not the major theme of the ode, is clearly referred to in the lines which follow.

From now on the imagery turns from that of the garden and the fruitful land to that of the tree, and in particular the Jesse tree. We have been thinking of Mary as the one in whom the praises of all creation gather. We pass to thinking of her as a topmost branch in the family tree of her own people. We think of the generations of faith and obedience, of struggle and dismay, which lie beyond the simple words of her acceptance of the divine calling. And the thought of the tree, which is primarily here a thought of fruitfulness, carries with it other associations, and we hear of a branch which is a cross which spreads peace abroad. We are confronted at the end of the canto with a sudden very specific image which anchors the whole in a moment of history. It is all 'a ferment' which ends with a Son in a Mother's lap.

We do not need to examine the third canto in the same detail as the first two. It is a slighter and less full exposition of its own great theme, the Holy Spirit coming to the Christian community, creating the community through baptism in which we are born again and become children of God and heirs of the Kingdom of heaven. As the poet says, 'the light/Gives life to us with its rich mystery'. Suffice it to say that as in Lancelot Andrewes, so here our birth by water and the Spirit in the Church is seen as rooted in the birth of the incarnate Christ for us. The font is the womb of the Church. At the end of the poem the fall hinted at earlier is mentioned explicitly, and the ode ends with a quiet prayer: 'May his grace go through us,/Rich to renew us,/A birth within us, and blessed are we.'

It is difficult, if not impossible, to imagine a contemporary poet in England who could handle such a subject with such technical assurance, and such explicitness and exuberance of affirmation. The contrast with the extreme reticence of Eliot in the *Four Quartets*, for instance, is very marked. We suspect that there is something, in the position of the poet in Wales, something maybe in the very nature of the Welsh language which makes this miracle possible. Perhaps the very fact that in some ways the Welsh language has been restricted in its use, so that while in poetry and theology it is rich, in other areas it is poor, has something to do with it. But perhaps what strikes us most about the poem, considered theologically, is its extraordinary power to fuse together into a single whole different levels and different moments. As Professor Hodges remarks, 'the subject of the ode is not the window, but genesis as signified in the window. But the two cannot be kept apart. The ferment of colour in the church becomes a ferment of ideas in the poet's mind, and in this again he sees the ferment of the divine activity.' The whole poem operates at many levels and yet all are drawn together into one.

As the poet himself expounds it, the ode is seen as a hymn to the creative, fruitful, healing light which proceeds from the Glory of the Eternal. It is, one might say, a poem about the divine energies, the uncreated grace, the gifts of the Spirit present and at work throughout creation – the light of God seen in the light of noonday and of evening as it shines through the changing colours of the window. It is a paean of praise to the divine Sophia, the wisdom and power of God at work in a ferment of birth throughout man's history.[3] This wisdom contains a principle of unity within itself which does not imply uniformity; a unity which is rooted in the particular, transforming but not obliterating it. Mary stands as the personification of the rooted, the singular, she who had her dwelling among her own people. It is in her that the unifying glory of the divine is made manifest. If we were to mention a twentieth-century theologian whose writing it suggests to us, we should incline rather to Bulgakov than to Barth or to Brunner. It is a poem which reaffirms the doctrine of man's creation in the image and likeness of his Maker, and which sees the work of incarnation and redemption as itself completed in a further coming, the coming of the Spirit in the Church. In such a vision it is not surprising that 'the fair one of the bright childbearing' should hold a central place, she to whom 'every province' of the Spirit's Kingdom pays homage. What may surprise us is the quiet assurance with which the poet sings the beauty of her humility. It is, moreover, he himself who has brought her into the centre of the picture, for while the font itself speaks of rebirth in baptism, and the window images the light of creation, the cathedral baptistery contains no explicit reference to the Blessed Virgin. Only the poet has made the connection, which sees her as the centre or type of the Church, a cup, a grail for the coming of the Spirit, the place where creation has received the fullness of the Godhead.

NOTES
1 The poem is to be found in the volume of poems by Euros Bowen entitled *Myfyrion* (Liverpool 1963), pp. 104–11. The poem is followed by three pages of notes and comments by the author from which these remarks are taken. I have made use of an unpublished translation by the late Professor H. A. Hodges, as also of his own most perceptive notes on the poem.
2 Dionysius the Areopagite, *On the Divine Names and The Mystical Theology*, trans. C. E. Rolt (London 1951), p. 106. But I have quoted

here the more accurate translation made by Andrew Louth for his work *The Origins of the Christian Mystical Tradition* (Oxford 1981), p. 176.

3 The Eastern Orthodox quality of the poem is surely not unrelated to the author's deep knowledge of the classical world of Greece and Rome. The Celtic tradition here rediscovers the relationship with the tradition of the Near East.

8

'The One Annunciation': Edwin Muir and T. S. Eliot

We have said in an earlier chapter that Christianity involves the meeting of time and eternity. Two 'todays', one temporal and one eternal, are united, fused into one. In the conjunction of apparent opposites the genuinely new comes to birth. God the eternal enters time, man the creature opens himself in an act of free and willing obedience. When this happens, time is fulfilled in being transcended, man's life begins to expand into its true and eternal dimensions.

In the twentieth century we live in a civilization which finds it particularly difficult to realize this mystery. Our society carries within itself a great weight of despair, a stifling sense of futility, because for us time seems to have become trapped within its own limiting dimensions. We deeply doubt whether this opening onto eternity is possible at all, or whether it can be more than a comforting illusion. The time sequence runs on inexorably and finds no fulfilment either within or beyond itself. Perhaps even, it is tied down to an iron rule of recurrence, so that everything that has happened once is bound to happen again, over and over again.

This at least was the fear of Edwin Muir, at the time when as a young man he was most strongly influenced by Nietzsche's idea of an eternal return. Throughout the whole of his life Muir was haunted by the mystery of time and eternity. If the intimations of immortality which he experienced so powerfully in his childhood, and which he describes with such vividness in the opening chapter of his *Autobiography*, were not true, if man were indeed a creature doomed to live and die in time alone, then he could only see himself and his fellow human beings as a random collection of dressed-up animals. He tells us of a frightening moment of vision when this thought came to him with an overpowering insistence. He wrote in his diary in 1939: 'Once long ago when I was sitting in a crowded tram-car in Glasgow, I was overcome by the feeling that all the people there were animals; a collection of animals all being borne along in a curious contrivance in a huge city where, far and wide, there was not an immortal soul. I did not believe in immortality at the time, and thought I was happy in my unbelief. . . But now I know that if you deny people immortality you deny them humanity.'[1]

This incident took place in his early manhood, when he was suffering the full effect of the shattering series of events which followed his family's move from the Orkneys, where he was born and grew up, into the slums of Edwardian Glasgow. As time went on, and particularly after his marriage, he began to come to himself, to recover his first vision, to discover the deeper meaning of his life and calling. He came to see that man's life in time is constantly touched by moments of eternity, and that these moments in which time and eternity meet are moments of redemption. In and through time, something from beyond time makes itself known and restores to time its meaning and direction. This process of rediscovery was for him a long and at times a painful one. But by the early 1940s it was coming to a climax, a climax which is recorded in a collection of poems called *The Narrow Place*, first published in 1943.

We can see this rediscovery in one of the poems in that book in which Muir draws on the matter of Scottish history, picturing the old heroic king Robert Bruce on his deathbed, haunted by the thought of Comyn's murder which had brought him to the throne, haunted by all the killing which had been involved in the necessary defence of his country's freedom. It is only in the cross of Christ that release can come from the endless repetition of such acts:

But that Christ hung upon the cross
    Comyn would rot until time's end
And bury my sin in boundless dust,
    For there is no amend

131

In order; yet in order run
　　All things in unreturning ways.
If Christ live not, nothing is there
　　For sorrow or for praise.[2]

This sense that in Christ's death there is a source of liberating forgiveness grew stronger in Muir as he grew older. It is expressed more fully in a poem written much later in his life, at a time when he was studying in Cambridge, Massachusetts. There he speaks of the cross as the place where God and man in more than love's embrace together suffer and die, so that a possibility of freedom is given to man, so that 'man will not *die in time, alone*'.[3] One has to have followed Muir's anguished conflict with the fear that man might live and die solely in time, to feel the full weight of those last simple but telling words.

In the Christian story, this process which finds its climax in the cross, begins at that moment when eternity greets time, which we call the annunciation. Muir was to write two poems with this title. The first of them follows closely on the poem about Robert Bruce and it is a very personal poem. For Muir a large part of the possibility of finding a way of liberation had been given through his relationship with his wife, his love for her, her love for him. They were very different people. She had much of the tough, outgoing quality which he, with his intense sensitivity to people and places, lacked. When you went to tea with them, it was she who came forward and did most of the talking, apparently taking the first place. Between them, in their mutual love, something very remarkable was given and received. So in this poem called 'The Annunciation', the love which is celebrated is their love for one another. Roger Knight, in his valuable and perceptive study of Muir's work, points out that this poem marks a definite turning point in Muir's development. After a long period of struggle and inner conflict something new appears. 'The "Annunciation" is the first poem of unqualified triumph, of escape from that reign (the "iron reign" of time and necessity, determination and death); the anguish, the yearning, the meditations have given way to a simple song, a song of celebration.'[4]

In the collection in which it appears, 'The Annunciation' is immediately followed by two other poems addressed to Willa Muir, which have the same radiantly happy quality: 'The Confirmation' and 'The Commemoration'. All three celebrate the gift of a relationship which time cannot unmake, a relationship in which each calls out in the other unrealized possibilities of good,

Each awakes in each
What else could never be.

They speak of the coming together of body and soul in a relationship which is healing and re-creative,

This is the most
That soul and body can
To make us each for each
And in our spirit whole.[5]

Commenting on these lines, Knight remarks on the simplicity and directness with which Muir speaks in these poems. 'Muir trusts words, trusts them as carriers of what matters to men, and he here calls upon them to give their natural shaping to a natural emotion. 'Soul', 'grace', 'spirit', 'pilgrimage': the ancient words are remade with a total absence of self-consciousness, a total faith in their power to express the nature of love between man and woman in an iron reign whose principal feature is that it denies the realities of which those words speak.'[6]

We are not surprised to learn that it was in the years when these poems were written that Muir had rediscovered the Christian faith which had always been hidden inside him. He tells us in his *Autobiography* how one evening as he was undoing his waistcoat buttons, while getting undressed, he found himself urgently repeating the Lord's Prayer, over and over again, and finding it full of inexhaustible meaning.[7] He was never to align himself with any particular Church. He stands on the edge of all of them, a radiant figure who puts a silent question mark against our pretensions to ecclesiastical exclusivism. Of the reality of his faith, there can be no doubt.

Muir's second poem called 'The Annunciation' dates from a period some years later, when he was for a time Director of the British Council's office in Rome. This was a time of no little importance in the development of his vision of the Christian faith.

In his childhood he had grown up in a pre-industrial world, in which the old seasonal rhythms of sowing and reaping and the care of animals were still very much alive. He liked to say of himself that he was born in 1750. But he had also grown up in a land which knew the all-pervasive influence of a kind of Christianity so afraid of symbols and images that in the end it seemed to deny the reality of the incarnation altogether.

The Word made flesh here is made word again,
a word made word in flourish and arrogant crook,
See here King Calvin with his iron pen,
And God three angry letters in a book,
And there the logical hook
On which the Mystery is impaled and bent
Into an ideological instrument.[8]

Euros Bowen, too, had known the influence of that type of religion. For him, as we have seen, the celebration of the Eucharist is itself the great safeguard against all temptations to make 'the Word of grace into an ideology of Christ'. The whole sacramental method of his poetic art is directly related to the central reality of the incarnation, which is made present in the Holy Communion. It is not for nothing that, among the works from the world of classical Greece and Rome which Bowen has translated into Welsh, there should be St Athanasius' treatise *On the Incarnation*. In him the theological connections are conscious and explicit.

Muir's approach is more intuitive. In Italy he could not but be aware of the fact that he was living in a society which had been centred on such sacramental acts. He was surrounded by the monuments of a civilization which had delighted to show forth the incarnation in visible form. 'You feel the gods (including the last and greatest of them) have all been here, and are still present in a sense in the places where once they were. It has brought very palpably to my mind the theme of incarnation, and I feel that probably I shall write a few poems on that high and difficult theme. . .' he wrote in a letter of December 1949.[9] In his *Autobiography* he notes: 'The cities of Tuscany and Umbria . . . looked like new incarnations sprung from the source of inexhaustible felicity, and though they had witnessed violence and crime, they rose above it into their own world and their own light.'[10]

One particular image struck him. It seemed to sum up much of what he was feeling. 'I remember stopping for a long time one day to look at a little plaque in the wall of a house in the Via degli Artisti, representing the annunciation. An angel and a young girl, their bodies inclined towards each other, their knees bent as if they were overcome by love, *'tutto tremante'*, gazed upon each other like Dante's pair; and that representation of a human love so intense that it could not reach further, seemed the perfect earthly symbol of the love that passes understanding.'[11] Muir, who had known so powerfully in his own life the creative, redeeming power of human love, sees in this image of such a relationship the perfect earthly symbol of a love divine, incomprehensible, unbounded.

> See, they have come together, see
> While the destroying minutes flow
> Each reflects the other's face
> Till heaven in hers, and earth in his
> Shine steady there. . .[12]

Time stands still in the moment of the intersection of the timeless with time. Here, as on the cross, we perceive that God and human-kind have come together 'in more than love's embrace'.

In the poem Muir describes both the messenger and the one to whom the message is addressed as caught up in 'an increasing rapture'. Knight comments at this point that here the poem departs from the gospel narrative of the annunciation; 'the persuasion of the poem is that the deepening trance is not supernatural; this love is human too.'[13] But Christianity is in no sense bound to the view that what is supernatural and what is natural are mutually exclusive. The central Christian tradition affirms that grace perfects nature and does not destroy it. Certainly this love is portrayed as human; but as Muir himself insists, it is seen as the embodiment of something which is more than human. True, such a depiction of the annunciation would, as Muir remarks, 'have shocked the congregations of the north, would have seemed a sort of blasphemy, perhaps an indecency'. But it need not seem so to a Christian faith which takes the principle of sacrament and image seriously.

The Fathers of the Church affirm that both in creation and redemption God comes out from himself in love. It is this 'mad love' of his, (the term is theirs not mine), which leads him for the sake of man to give himself to death on the cross. We have seen in the preceding chapter how Dionysius speaks of God's coming out from himself in love and longing for his creation. Such an intensity of love on God's part is clearly hinted at already in the Old Testament, and especially in the prophets and the Psalms. 'The Lord hath chosen Sion to be an habitation for himself; he has longed for her' (Psalm 132). When such words are applied to Mary, the daughter of Sion, the personification of the Holy City, it hardly seems inappropriate to speak of the angel's 'increasing rapture'. Indeed the Eastern Christian tradition, which has spoken more freely of man's entering into the life of God and God entering into the life of man, affirms that as man increases in the knowledge and the love of God, so God's joy in man increases and deepens.

To speak, as Muir does here, of the angel's 'increasing rapture' is only to speak in a bold and figurative way of the depth and intensity of God's love for man, which is presupposed in the very thought of divine incarnation. So again when Roger Knight speaks of the poem as being, for better or worse, other than Christian, because 'it perfectly represents Muir's feeling that incarnation is not a possession of the specifically Christian imagination, still less is it limited to *the* incarnation', it seems to me that he is pointing to those very qualities which make the poem so profoundly and triumphantly Christian. It represents a Christianity which knows that the mystery of the incarnation is not the *possession* of the mind or the imagination of Christendom. As F. D. Maurice says, the truth of God is not something which we hold, it is something which holds us. The word of grace is not an ideology of Christ. It also represents a Christianity which knows that the principle of incarnation is not limited to *the* incarnation. It finds its inclusive and not exclusive centre there. 'The Word of God, who is God, wills always and in all things to work the mystery of his embodiment', as Maximus the Confessor declares. This is the Christianity which we have been exploring throughout this book, a Christianity which may rightly call itself catholic. This annunciation proclaims the joy of *all* creation.

How far such thoughts were explicitly in the mind of Edwin Muir is another matter. In his humility he seems at times to have been unaware of how deeply Christian his imagination was. This is certainly the case with the opening sections of his poem called 'The Transfiguration'. It was only after its publication that he discovered that his vision of the world, as transfigured in the presence of Christ, corresponds to one of the major themes of Eastern Christian thought and devotion. What seems clear, however, is that in his poetry Muir received the gift to express in unforgettable ways something of the mystery both of *the* incarnation, and of an incarnation, for a time in which such thoughts do not come easily.

Muir's first poem called 'The Annunciation' was, as we have seen, addressed to his wife. In a later volume, *The Labyrinth* (1949) he addressed two further poems to her, 'Love's Remorse' and 'Love in Time's Despite' in which he expresses more clearly than anywhere else his faith that through fidelity and love we are enabled to share in a reality which is greater than that of time, a reality whose roots are in the realm of the eternal.

> And we who love and love again can dare
> To keep in (time's) despite our summer still
> Which flowered, but shall not wither, at his will.[14]

Here in what is most intimate and personal something sure and lasting is given and received.

If for Edwin Muir the sense of the destructiveness of time could be an overwhelming and insupportable burden, how much more so was this the case with T. S. Eliot. For Eliot, unlike Muir, was entirely a man of our own age. Muir had always at his back the memory of the pre-industrial world of his boyhood, a world in which ballads and legends, folk songs and folk tales were still alive, in which it was still possible to speak directly of the world of men and the gods. 'The Orkney I was born into was a place where there was no great distinction between the ordinary and the fabulous; the lives of living men turned into legend.'[15] In Eliot on the other hand we feel the full force of the darkness of our age. It is one of the things which makes him able to speak so clearly on our behalf.

It is this, of course, which is set out in *The Waste Land*. There above all we see the sense of the futility which besets a time which finds itself unredeemed by anything beyond time.

> A crowd flowed over London Bridge, so many,
> I had not thought death had undone so many.[16]

How was it that for Eliot redemption came? At the personal level, in ways altogether different from those followed by Edwin Muir. But at the level of their understanding of the inner and permanent content of redemption, there is a curious similarity between the two men, all the more striking because of the great differences between them, both as writers and human beings. For Eliot too there is the discovery that here in time eternity makes itself known, the discovery that God has entered into our flesh, into the very substance of human history, taking the initiative and opening the way for man to go forward, to rediscover hope, even to be born again. The way of the discovery of faith is always a discovery of hope, a slow and painful process, often tentative and groping. For Eliot the thought of Mary is not absent from that process. We find it hinted at more than once in 'Ash Wednesday'. There the Beatrice-like figure who intercedes for the poet is said to 'honour the Virgin in meditation'. Indeed when she is invoked 'Blessed sister, holy mother', she seems almost to merge with her. And the thought of Mary's prayer for us is explicitly evoked in the words from the 'Salva Regina' which occur at the end of section iv.

But it is in his last poetic work, *Four Quartets*, that we find the fullest exploration of this theme of the relation of eternity to time, and the most direct and unambiguous invocation of our Lady. Already in the opening lines of the first of the *Quartets*, 'Burnt Norton', the question of time present and time past in relation to time future has been announced. Already we are presented with the futility and sadness of a time which knows only the dimensions of before and after, and can see no further than that.

> Here is a place of disaffection
> Time before and time after
> In a dim light . . .

And as if to underline the repetitiveness of such an experience of life, the line

Time before and time after

is itself repeated a few lines further on. Time unredeemed by glimpses of eternity can never be more than

Ridiculous the waste sad time
Stretching before and after.[17]

These themes are more fully developed in the third of the series, 'The Dry Salvages'. In this poem the dominant element is water; the sea provides the leading image. In the first section we hear the menacing but ambiguous clamour of the sea bell. It is worth remarking that Samuel Eliot Morison, the distinguished American historian of the sea, who better than most knew the coast of Massachusetts to which this poem constantly refers, insists on the extreme accuracy of Eliot's recall of the different sea sounds described in this passage. We are dealing here not with unrelated fantasy, but with acute observation and with real bodily images.

The tolling bell
Measures time not our time, rung by the unhurried
Ground swell, a time
Older than the time of chronometers. . .

This time, which is other than ours, is something to which we shall come back. For the moment, however, the tolling bell inevitably suggests death, and so we hear of

. . .anxious worried women
Lying awake, calculating the future,
Trying to unweave, unwind, unravel
And piece together the past and the future,
Between midnight and dawn, when the past is all deception,
The future futureless, before the morning watch
When time stops and time is never ending.

There could hardly be a more perfect description of a time unilluminated by hope, in which the present has been squeezed out of existence by a past which is all deception, and by a future which is futureless, a moment in which time stops, and yet time is never ending. As in many places, so here, Eliot speaks of a universal condition in terms of a particular predicament. Is not our whole civilization, with its unacknowledged anxiety about nuclear warfare, with its loss of any living sense of tradition, at times caught up in a mood such as this, where the past has become an illusion, the future without issue? It is in such a situation that

> the ground swell, that is and was from the beginning,
> Clangs
> The bell.

There follows one of the most amazing of all Eliot's technical achievements, the sequence of six six-lined stanzas, in which in each stanza the corresponding lines rhyme throughout the passage. As a piece of poetic virtuosity it stands comparison with the eighty lines of monorhymed *cynghanedd* with which Euros Bowen begins his great ode. There is a technical perfection which corresponds to the sureness with which what is said, is said. Here the stanzas express the sadness of a world which knows no redemption, where all things necessarily and inevitably lead towards death. The very rhyme words chosen are eloquent in this regard; for instance, wailing, trailing, failing, or motionless, devotionless, oceanless, or wreckage, breakage, leakage, wastage.

> Where is there an end of it, the soundless wailing
> The silent withering of autumn flowers. . . ?

> There is no end, but addition: the trailing
> Consequence of further days and hours,
> While emotion takes to itself emotionless
> Years of living among the breakage
> Of what was believed in as the most reliable. . .

> There is the final addition, the failing
> Pride or resentment at failing powers. . .
> The silent listening to the undeniable
> Clamour of the bell of the last annunciation.

We have, the poet says, to think of our seamen as 'forever bailing'. The life of mankind must go on; we cannot all the time face the certainty of the end. There is in man an amazing resilience, an unsuspected courage. We continue to strive, 'forever bailing', but it is in 'a drifting boat with a slow leakage'. And in the end there is only one issue.

There is no end of it, the voiceless wailing,
No end to the withering of withered flowers,
To the movement of pain that is painless and motionless,
To the drift of the sea and the drifting wreckage,
The bone's prayer to Death its God. Only the hardly, barely
    prayable
Prayer of the one Annunciation.[18]

The force with which we receive the sudden and unexpected denouement, the weight of the last two lines, tells us how much Eliot wishes us to ponder the meaning of the one annunciation. Here, at a moment when we had been driven beyond faith and beyond hope, there appears a way through; here there is a moment which can change the direction and the significance of all that has gone before, of all that follows after, the moment in which the proffer of eternity is met with the fullness of the response of time. In the response of the one who receives the angelic greeting, all is restored, renewed.

In the context of such a reversal, brought about in the moment in which eternity, in the person of the angel, comes to greet our world of time, we can see that the medieval Latin play on the words *Ave* and *Eva* – the word of the angelic greeting, the name of our first mother – is something more than a mere play on words. Eva is the name which signifies life, for in Genesis Eve is called the mother of all living. But this is life lived towards death; it is this movement towards death which is reversed by the word of heavenly greeting, a word which is full of the Spirit, Creator and Life-giver. This is a greeting which, by bringing into being a new and direct relationship between man and God, conveys eternal life to humankind. Thus the life towards death, the life which we all inherit from our ancestors, is changed into a life which through death opens out into hitherto unsuspected possibilities of life. With such words of love and rescue, the Kingdom of eternity comes out to greet the children of time.

141

In this context we can see too that the association which the poets of Wales in the Middle Ages liked to make between the words *Ave* and *Awen*, the Welsh word for the poetic muse, which in that tradition is often considered a direct gift of the Holy Spirit, is also something more than fanciful. In his study of the religious significance of the Welsh literary tradition, Professor Bobi Jones argues that the work of the poet in itself involves a kind of incarnation, a making specific, a giving flesh to what is eternal and universal. The poetic image binds together the seen with the unseen, the limited with what is infinite. By his art the writer restores to words their fullness of meaning; can indeed show us that all our words are rooted in the One who is himself the Word, in whom is the fullness of all meaning.[19] But this power to give birth to the word is always a gift which comes to him. He is to receive an annunciation. The poetic word only becomes creative and life-giving in so far as it is inhabited by the Creator Spirit. It can then become a means by which the lives of men and women are liberated into dimensions larger than those of time. The greeting which the poet or the artist conveys to us is one that he must himself have received. As C. G. Jung says, 'Man is never helped in his suffering by what he thinks for himself, but only by revelations of a wisdom greater than his own. It is this which lifts him out of his distress.'[20] A large part of the poet's craft consists in learning how to be receptive and obedient. We have seen how this was the case both for Muir and for Eliot, and how it is that through them, it may be so for us. We are not surprised that in both men, despite the very great difference between them, the thought of the one annunciation should become so crucial. In the 'iron reign' of the century in which we live, we may feel a special sense of personal indebtedness to such men whose words of greeting can restore our courage to be, at times when we had lost all courage.

In the section of Eliot's poem which follows we are referred to the greatest of the Hindu scriptures, the Bhagavad Gita; we hear about Krishna and Arjuna on the field of battle. This reference to another religious tradition is full of significance here. The change in human history marked by the one annunciation is of universal import. It works backwards as well as forwards in time. It is by no means confined to Christendom. And what is of particular

142

relevance to the theme of redemption is the teaching of Krishna about the moment of death; 'on whatsoever sphere of being the mind of man may be intent at the time of death – that is the one action (*and the time of death is every moment*) which shall fructify in the lives of others'. We may learn to live fruitfully, allowing the present its proper fullness, if we learn to realize that the time of death is every moment. We are to live each day, each hour as if it were our last, because in fact it is our last. At every moment, whether we like it or not, we have died to some element of life which will never return. Time itself, even though we may measure it with our chronometers, is finally not ours to control. There is a time which is not ours, which belongs to God. This is the time by which ultimately our lives are measured. And for this very reason the possibility is always open that we shall die not into death, but into life, accepting for ourselves the call of the one annunciation. The bell which heralds death may become the bell which announces the message of the angel.

At this point the fourth section intervenes with its serene and simple invocation:

Lady, whose shrine stands on the promontory,
Pray for all those who are in ships, those
Whose business has to do with fish, and
Those concerned with every lawful traffic
And those who conduct them.

Repeat a prayer also on behalf of
Women who have seen their sons or husbands
Setting forth, and not returning:
Virgine madre, figlia del tuo figlio,
Queen of heaven.

Also pray for those who were in ships, and
Ended their voyage on the sand, in the sea's lips
Or in the dark throat which will not reject them
Or wherever cannot reach them the sound of the sea bell's
Perpetual angelus.[21]

At first sight, after the anguish which has preceded them, these quiet lines, asking Mary to pray both for the living and the dead, may seem almost prosaic, banal, 'all those who are in ships, those whose business has to do with fish'. Billingsgate, we remember, is also part of the city of London. Suddenly having turned the corner of prayer, having arrived in harbour, everything seems quiet, human, ordinary. This return to normality, this rediscovery of earth, rather than the storming of heaven, is reminiscent of a strangely moving poem of Edwin Muir's, 'The Good Man in Hell'. In it the writer speculates about what would happen if by an error in the celestial bureaucracy, a good man were to be confined in hell. Would he join the general chorus of recrimination and hatred, or would he even there succeed in retaining hope and faith – even in hell? And if he did, what would happen? The whole structure of hatred and despair would gradually disintegrate.

> One doubt of evil would bring down such a grace
> Open such a gate, all Eden would enter in,
> Hell be a place like any other place,
> And love and hate and life and death begin.[22]

The insidious power of good is enough to undermine the whole contraption of evil. Suddenly life begins again; not heaven, but this world in its complexity, its mixture of good and evil, its space for human freedom. Even one doubt of evil allows the grace of God to enter in, and entering to make all things different. Muir's poem was published in January 1938. One might call it prophetic, so clearly does it foreshadow the reports which have come to us from the hells of Nazi Germany and Soviet Russia, in the works of writers like Alexander Solzhenitsyn, Sinyavsky or Ginsburg, accounts of the power of naked goodness over against the might of organized evil, to restore a dignity and inner freedom to man, even in the most extreme circumstances.

So in the poem of Eliot's, to find the possibility of faith, to be able to open a way for the grace of God to enter in, does not in some magic way resolve all problems. It enables us to enter a world in which it becomes possible to believe in, and even to foresee, their resolution.

In this passage, for all its apparent simplicity, there is much that demands further investigation. 'Lady, whose shrine stands on the *promontory*'; Gregory Palamas, the greatest theologian of the later

Middle Ages in the Christian East, speaks of our Lady as being herself the *methorion*, the threshold, the boundary between earth and heaven. John Keble speaks of a position 'on this side touching sin, on the other heaven'. In his commentary on the *Four Quartets*, Harry Blamires remarks of this word that 'it reminds us that the Virgin's place (historic and philosophic) is at the point where the land whose soil is the nourishment and end of life in the flesh, juts out – into the waters, whose nearer waves are the waves of time, but whose further reaches represent the sea of eternity.'[23]

No less significant is the sudden and explicit quotation from Dante: *Virgine madre, figlia del tuo figlio*, Virgin Mother, daughter of thy Son, which brings into the poem the whole wealth of Dante's own vision of Mary, and his understanding of the affirmative way through his love for Beatrice. This direct quotation, it is suggested, 'injects into the poem a concentrated fusion of allusive overtones which oblique and less readily identifiable literary echoes establish only gradually'. The ordinary allusions, which Eliot uses so often, correspond to 'the fitful, particular, experiential hints of an eternal intersecting a temporal order'. This kind of direct citation sends us back to 'the decisive archetypal act of divine Incarnation, of which the Virgin Mary is the instrument. . . In this movement the figure of the Virgin Mary is before us as the one whose Annunciation is the pattern of all human vocations to self-sacrifice, whose obedient response should be the pattern of all human responses to vocational demands'.[24] By her free response she opens the way towards the fullness of incarnation and redemption. This is the beginning of that work of God's grace which will turn the tolling bell of the first part of the poem into the perpetual angelus with which this section ends. In the annunciation made to Mary, and in her obedient and willing reply, all the mystery of man's liberation from frustration and death is foreshadowed and contained.

This truth can be seen in the very form of the devotion called 'the angelus', to which Eliot refers. It is a form of prayer familiar throughout Catholic Christendom and certainly one which must have been often in Eliot's own heart and mind. To announce it the church bell is rung first of all in three groups of three strokes; and then, after a pause, in nine strokes together. The first group of three commemorates the angelic salutation, 'The angel of the Lord brought tidings to Mary and she conceived by the Holy Ghost.' The second group commemorates her response, 'Behold the handmaid of the Lord, be it unto me according to thy word.' The third tells us of the immeasurable consequence, 'The Word was made flesh and dwelt among us.' And each time the believer adds his own salutation which is also a request for prayer, 'Hail Mary, full of grace, the Lord is with thee, blessed art thou among women and blessed is the fruit of thy womb Jesus. Holy Mary, Mother of God, pray for us sinners now and at the hour of our death.' Then come the nine strokes of the bell which are accompanied by the following prayer, which is, as it happens, the collect for the feast of the Annunciation: 'Grant, O Lord, that as we have known the incarnation of thy Son Jesus Christ, through the message of an angel, so by his cross and passion we may be brought unto the glory of his resurrection.'

In this form of prayer we hold together in one the thought of the birth of the saviour at Bethlehem with the thought of his dying and rising again in Jerusalem, the present moment of the believer's life, now, with the final moment, the hour of his death, which is already latent in that present moment. We bring together the Saviour's birth and dying with our own. The barely prayable prayer of the one annunciation becomes the type of all human acts of faith and obedience in response to the divine initiative, even of that supreme act which Mary's Son is to make at the moment when he offers himself to death, and in doing so overcomes death.

We begin to see why it is that the moment of the annunciation is the moment which makes sense of all other moments. It is a moment which is truly in time, not out of time. It has a whole series of temporal consequences; the embryo begins to stir in the womb. But it is a moment in which eternity has really come, in which God is present and at work. Both the birth and the death of Jesus witness to the depth and immensity of God's love, and to the infinite openness and potential of human life. And just as, in baptism, the death of each one who is baptized is included in Christ's death, in order that the whole process of dying may become dying into life, so also the birth of each one is included in Christ's birth, in order that the whole process of living may be open to the coming of the Spirit, who is Lord and giver of life. Grundtvig expresses this magnificently in a verse in which he says

Each one has his own birthday
For this world's affairs
For struggle and defeat
And ultimately for death.
But for life and peace and joy
Christmas night with the angels' songs
Is the hour of our birth.[25]

It is in this sense that we may rightly think of Mary as the mother of us all; in this sense that Andrewes speaks of the font as the womb of the Church, of one substance with the Virgin's womb, with a power given it by the Spirit of bringing forth sons of God. From his participation in our human nature follows our participation in his divine nature. The life of eternity enters into time, so that the life of time may find its fulfilment in eternity.

Considerations such as these show us that there is a closer relationship between faith in the Virgin birth and faith in the bodily resurrection of Christ than might at first sight appear. Both doctrines affirm the depth of God's love, the extent of his involvement in the human mass, in the very substance of our human history, its reality of flesh and blood. And both doctrines affirm the potential greatness, the infinite openness of that human history. In the reality of flesh and blood, the eternal is made present and made known. It is not surprising that our own society, with its sense of being held in an 'iron reign' of necessity and death, with its particular difficulty in believing that human life can open out into something larger than itself, finds these doctrines difficult to accept. In some sense, however, this has always been the case, for at all times these articles of faith have brought a judgement on our fallen ways of thinking. They are bound to come to our minds first as a cross and only afterwards as a fulfilment.

But it is of fulfilment that both ultimately speak, for while both tell of a mystery given from on high, they also speak of the fulfilment of what is given from below. Neither Christ's conception nor his rising again is an isolated wonder, unrelated to the rest of human history, to the nature of the universe as a whole. 'The truth, which is revealed in them, is at the same time situated at the heart of history, at the basis of creation and at the goal of history.'[26] All stories of strange or miraculous births, and there are many in the legends and mythology of man, hint at the potential of a birth from above, at the mystery of each human life as a new creation, a possible point of the intersection of the timeless with time. The point is well made by Alwyn Rees in his book *The Celtic Heritage*.[27] All stories of a return from death, or even perhaps of an inexplicable escape from death, hint at the potential of a fully human death, which would be a death in which our understanding of death was changed rather than our understanding of the one who had died, in which death would be included in something greater than itself. In this sense the death of Socrates and of St Francis, for all the differences, show us something of what such a death might be.

The birth and death of Christ, given from on high, are a full and perfect confirmation of these half-lost human longings. They are at one and the same time a revelation of the mysteriousness of the divine love which goes far beyond anything the mind could have thought or the heart desired, and also a revelation of the mysteriousness of the human calling and destiny. Planted at the heart of man's being there is an openness to what is beyond him.

> These events stand at the apex of supernatural revelation, but at the same time they are events of the complete restoration of nature to its condition and destiny as nature, that is to say, as the place where the Spirit is made manifest unhindered. For this very reason they foreshadow the restoration of the whole of nature to its true being at the end of time, when the Spirit will rejoice in a full and eternal victory. . .[28]

Thus in Christ it is revealed that both at birth and at death, man's life can conquer time through time. The moments which in themselves can be and are the perfect symbols of man's bondage to time and of his imprisonment in a world of endless recurrence, birth, copulation and death, become the very symbols of man's liberation from death, and of the liberation of all creation. This is not only a liberation from the cycle of birth and death, it is a liberation through them by the taking up of time into eternity. She who stands at the entrance to this mystery, the place where the Spirit is made manifest, is indeed the gate of heaven, the joy of all creation.

NOTES
1   P. H. Butter, *Edwin Muir, Man and Poet* (Edinburgh 1966), p. 51
2   Edwin Muir, *Collected Poems* (1960), p. 115
3   Ibid., p. 263
4   Roger Knight, *Edwin Muir, an Introduction to his Work* (1980), p. 120
5   Ibid., p. 117.
6   Ibid., p. 121
7   Edwin Muir, *An Autobiography* (1969), p. 246
8   Op. cit., p. 228
9   *Selected Letters of Edwin Muir*, ed. P. H. Butler (1974), p. 154
10 Op. cit., p. 279
11 Ibid., p. 278
12 Op. cit., p. 223
13 Knight, p. 193
14 Op. cit., p. 193
15 Quoted in Knight, p. 10. In this respect his years in the Orkneys gave him an experience which he shares with some of his Welsh-language contemporaries, who in the linguistic community in which they grew up had access to resources not easily available to the twenti-eth-century poet writing in English. In their work we find a similar capacity for direct and unironic statement of traditional truths.
16 T. S. Eliot, *The Waste Land*
17 'Burnt Norton'
18 'The Dry Salvages'
19 R. M. Jones, *Llen Cymru a Chrefydd* (Abertawe 1978), p. 210 and pp. 53–4
20 Quoted in Knight, p. 100
21 'The Dry Salvages'
22 Op. cit., p. 104
23 Harry Blamires, *Word Unheard: A Guide Through Eliot's 'Four Quartets'* (1969), p. 110
24 Ibid.
25 N. F. S. Grundtvig, *Sang-Vaerk*, vol. i. (Copenhagen 1949), p. 419
26 John D. Zizioulas, 'Vérité et Communion' in *Irenikon* (1977) no. 4, pp. 451–510. Page 484, resuming the thought of Maximus the Confessor
27 Alwyn Rees and Brinley Rees, *Celtic Heritage* (1961)
28 Maximus the Confessor, *Philosophical and Theological Questions*, vol.

1. Introduction and Commentary by Father Staniloae. (Athens 1978, in modern Greek), p. 50

Epilogue

At the beginning of this book we remarked on the way in which what is universal in Christianity is rooted in what is particular, made known in specific times and specific places. This theme has pursued us throughout our inquiry, and it has led us to see Mary as herself the embodiment of this principle, the one in whom the uncontainable is contained. 'Here', as Mark Frank says, 'is the shrine and altar, the glorious Virgin's lap, where the Saviour of the world is laid to be worshipped and adored.'

It is not therefore surprising to find that in Christian history Mary's name has been linked with innumerable holy places. It was one of the complaints of the Reformers. There were so many 'ladies'; our Lady of this and our Lady of that. 'She's a rare one for locality', as David Jones, writer and artist, puts it. This aspect of the mystery of Mary is one on which Pope John Paul seems to love to dwell, drawing out in his speeches the multiplicity of the places which are linked with her name. In his visit to Mexico in 1979, at the shrine of our Lady of Guadalupe he said: 'No less has been your presence in other places, where your children invoke you with tender names, as our Lady of Altagracie, of the Aparecida, of Lujon, and with many other no less affectionate names, not to give an unending list, names by which in each nation and even in each region the peoples of Latin America express their devotion.'[1]

She it is who, by her vocation to be the place of God, and by her fulfilment of that vocation, reveals the true destiny of all places, indeed of all humankind and all creation, which shares in that high calling to become the place of God's inhabitation. This again is why she is called the joy of all creation, because the whole creation finds its possibility of fulfilment in her. If, as we thought in the previous chapter, all moments of time are touched and, as it were, redeemed, by the moment of the one annunciation, so too all the places where men dwell are touched and potentially opened to the divine indwelling by her acceptance of the angelic salutation. The very nature of time and space is illumined and transformed when the divine presence is made known within it.

And because it is seen in her that this world is capable of becoming the place of God, so again it becomes possible to see it as the place of man. For it is only when this world is known as God's world that it can become the true dwelling-place of human-kind. In her this world reveals its true quality, as the good earth, the land of promise, the place where God's blessing descends in its fullness. When man ceases to try to hold onto this world as his own exclusive possession, when he ceases to devour it with unmeasured greed, when he acknowledges it as God's gift to him to be held in trust for future generations, then he is able to receive it and rejoice in it, as his rightful inheritance. 'Blessed are the meek, for they shall inherit the earth' (Matt. 5:5). The promise of the second beatitude takes on all its meaning in this context. Behind it lies the assurance of the psalmist, 'those who wait for the Lord shall possess the land. . . The meek shall possess the land and enjoy the abundance of peace' (Ps. 37:9, 11). An attitude of contemplative openness and delight before the gifts of God, a recognition of our own creaturely limitations and fragility, above all a certain awe and respect before the mysteries of existence, – these are the attitudes which receive the abundance of the divine blessing. Only in the rediscovery of such attitudes, which are symbolized in the person of Mary, and which have been highly valued not only in Christianity but in many of the religious traditions of mankind, shall we begin to find a resolution of the urgent ecological problems which confront us, as a result of our inhuman rapacity and greed.

The good earth which we inherit is above all the good earth of our own bodies. And it is here that we begin to see how it is that the mystery of Mary responds to and hallows the most basic elements of our common human experience. For if man is a journey, woman is a place. It is the mother who creates the home, transforms an anonymous dwelling area into the place where a family can grow and develop, a place which becomes filled with memories and associations, in which the very things that make it up, and not only the people who live there, are known and loved, cared for and remembered. She does this primarily simply by being there, by her bodily presence, and then by the quality of that presence, 'welcoming and forgiving, praying and receiving, obedient and compassionate, confident and joyful'.[2]

The lives of all of us begin in the body of our mother. We are related to that place, that piece of the material world, in a way in which we are related to no other place. For most of us our first experience of food comes in relation to that body. It is there that we learn to eat and are initiated into the community of eating and drinking, which provides so many of the basic structures of all human community. For most of us our first experience of speech is no less intimately, and only slightly less physically, connected with the body of our mother. This is where our insertion into the community of language, of shared speaking and singing, listening and attending has its origins. When we reflect on facts like these in relation to the human development of Jesus, we begin to see more of the hidden reasons for the tradition of devotion to his mother. As a former Archbishop of Canterbury says about the way in which Jesus learnt to pray, 'So we watch Mother and Son at prayer, and in doing so we tread on holy ground.'[3]

The implications of all this are numberless. To take a single example from a statement made by the bishops of Poland in May 1978, about the duties of Christians towards their nation and its inheritance, 'One can suppose that the deepest of all foundations of national culture is to be found in the word of the mother which gives birth to the child's first smile. From that moment onwards, he is inserted ever more deeply into the great poem of the language of his nation, which grows stronger in the consciousness of the child, the youth, the adult, the speaker, the writer. . .'[4] Similarly in baptism, in which we receive our Christian name, God's word is spoken to us and draws out our response, bringing us into the great poem of the sacramental action of the universal Church. There we are reborn to new and eternal life. There we find that the

153

natural communities of eating and drinking, of speaking and singing provide the basic structures which in Christ and in the Spirit are taken up and transformed, so as to acquire eternal significance and power.

The Church itself is built up around the common meal in which all divisions are transcended, in which men and women are reconciled with one another because together reconciled with God, in which they find that they can share the good things of this earth with all their fellow human beings, because all are acknowledged as children of a common Father. The gift of speech, which in the fragmentation of human language has become divisive, a source of constant separation, in the event of Pentecost is itself healed and restored. In the gift of the Spirit from on high, the tongues of humankind, in all their diversity, are united in a common sacrifice of praise and thanksgiving. In the joy which comes from God, love and knowledge unite to open our hearts and minds to one another, to make possible a new creation in the Spirit, and thus to make of this earth the dwelling-place of a single family.

None of these things is done without the body. All have their roots in the simplest of our physical needs and actions. As Jeremy Taylor remarks about the breastfeeding of babies, 'Although other actions are more perfect and spiritual, yet this is more natural and humane; other things . . . rise higher, but this builds stronger and is like a part of the foundation, having no lustre, but much strength.' So in the mosaics of the birth and childhood of Mary, which fill the narthex of the church of St Saviour in Chora in Istanbul with colour and delight, we see the joy of parents in their children, of children in their parents as the basis of the whole future development of man's salvation.

Thus it is that wherever she is made known, whether at Czestochowa in Poland or at Tinos in Greece, at Chartres in France or at Zeitoun in Egypt, at Knock in Ireland or at Guadalupe in Mexico, Mary is made known as one who gives life and courage to a whole people, and particularly to an oppressed people. She is one in whom powers and dominations are brought down and the insignificance of the humble is exalted; one who makes of this world a place of man's, no less than of God's, habitation.

And this which is true in many lands, is true also in England.

Here is the significance behind the simple yet mysterious command which, in the eleventh century, came to the Lady Richeldis, to build a copy of the holy house at Walsingham, so that that place might become England's Nazareth. Walsingham became in the Middle Ages one of the greatest of English places of pilgrimage. From every part of the country people came to greet Mary in this place which she had made her own. Is it surprising that among the most poignant of all sixteenth-century melodies should be one called 'Walsingham', the tune sung to the words which lament the destruction of this holy place? For centuries Walsingham, like so many other places of pilgrimage in Great Britain, lay desolate and neglected. Then in our own century, almost without people noticing it, something began to change. The holy places stirred into new life. Once again men and women came to Iona, Glastonbury, Canterbury, Walsingham and found God's healing peace and presence there.

We have remarked in previous chapters that the age in which we live is not one which finds it easy to believe in the mystery of the Word made flesh, and that is true. But it is also true that in this late and unpropitious time, God's grace, as always, is at work healing what is wounded, making up what is lacking in his creation. If for the scholars and the theologians this has been a time when they have found it difficult to speak of Mary, the people of the Church seem to have been given a new boldness to sing her praises and to rejoice in calling her blessed.

John Keble in the nineteenth century, faced with new threats to the faith which he had inherited from his father, found a new freedom and a new openness in his approach to Mary. So in our own century the unselfconscious and joyful faith of those who have flocked to Walsingham in ever increasing numbers has made its own eloquent response to the mood of despondency and faithlessness which has at times assailed the Church, and which reveals itself on both sides of many of our current controversies; in those who suggest that unless everything can be kept just as it is the Church will collapse, no less than in those who imply that unless everything can be reformed according to the latest recipe, there is no future for the Christian religion. Both attitudes reflect a fundamental lack of faith in God. Both suggest that he depends on us. The truth, as Mary teaches us, is exactly the reverse. We depend on him. He rules in the affairs of men. It is only as we grow in that faith that the Church will be able to become, with Mary, truly 'welcoming and forgiving, praying and receiving, obedient and compassionate, confident and joyful'.

Who would have believed at the beginning of this century that Walsingham would again become a national centre of pilgrimage, and a place of great ecumenical influence, attracting Roman Catholics and Orthodox, as well as Anglicans and Christians of other traditions? Who in the early years of Fr Hope Patten's pioneering struggle to restore the shrine would have believed that within fifty years an Archbishop of Canterbury would again come to Walsingham, and would preach and preside at the great Whitsuntide pilgrimage? In his sermon on 26 May 1980, the Archbishop spoke of the essential meaning of Mary's example: 'We live in a society which trusts overmuch in words, organization, activism. Mary reminds us that quietness, longing, receptivity to the Word of God are the beginnings of growth in the Gospel.'[5] In the light of such words spoken on such an occasion, we may think that the hidden stream of thought and prayer which we have charted in these pages and which has flowed almost unnoticed through the Anglican tradition during these last four centuries, has been more deeply influential than most have suspected. Perhaps it is now, as Anglicans begin to be drawn into unity with those from whom too long they have been separated, that there will break out a new song of praise to her in whom the whole creation turns to God and finds in him the unexpected, the unbelievable joy of its fulfilment.

NOTES
1 *John Paul II in Mexico: His Collected Speeches* (1979), p. 42
2 Words from the sermon by the Archbishop of Canterbury at Walsingham on 26 May 1980
3 Donald Coggan, *The Prayers of the New Testament* (1974), p. 48
4 In *La Documentation catholique*, no. 1742, 21 May 1978, p. 462
5 Op. cit.

Dramatis Personae

1   **Lancelot Andrewes** (1555–1626). Successively bishop of Chichester, Ely and Winchester. Scholar, theologian, controversialist, preacher, man of prayer. One of the most important influences in the formation of the Anglican tradition.

2   **Euros Bowen** (1904–   ). One of the most distinguished poets writing in Welsh today; has published many volumes of verse, including one bilingual volume in 1976. Also translator of Sophocles, Virgil and Athanasius. Formerly Rector of Langywair on the shores of Lake Bala.

3   **S. T. Coleridge** (1772–1834). Poet, critic and thinker. His influence was pervasive in the religious thought of the nineteenth century. But it is only recently that the full scope of this thought is being realized through publication of his notebooks and papers.

4   **T. S. Eliot** (1888–1965). Poet and critic; born in America, he lived and worked in England. By common consent one of the greatest writers in English of our time. Baptized into the Church in 1926, for many years churchwarden of St Stephen's, Gloucester Road, London.

5   **Richard Field** (1561–1616). Dean of Gloucester, intimate friend of Richard Hooker. His treatise *Of the Church* is one of the fullest discussions of ecclesiology from an Anglican author.

6   **Mark Frank** (1613–64). Master of Pembroke College, Cambridge. Preacher and theologian, friend of the Ferrars

at Little Gidding. The article in the *Dictionary of National Biography* describes his sermons as 'plain, sensible and evangelical discourses'.

7 **Nikolai Frederick Severin Grundtvig** (1784–1873). Dane of Danes, preacher, prophet, priest, poet, politician, scholar and educationalist. With Søren Kierkegaard, from whom he differs completely, the greatest figure of the Danish Church in his time. Decidedly not an Anglican.

8 **Reginald Heber** (1783–1826). Bishop of Calcutta from 1823 to 1826. Hymn writer and scholar of the Evangelical school. Best known for his Trinity hymn, 'Holy, holy, holy.'

9 **George Herbert** (1593–1633). Poet, son of a noble family, Public Orator in the University of Cambridge. Rejected preferment in Church or state to become vicar of the parish of Bemerton near Salisbury. Author of *The Temple* and *A Priest to the Temple*.

10 **Richard Hooker** (1554–1600). Greatest Anglican theologian since the Reformation. Master of the Temple Church in London, then Rector of Bishopsbourne near Canterbury. Wrote *The Laws of Ecclesiastical Polity*; learned, irenic, comprehensive.

11 **Fenton John Anthony Hort** (1828–92). Friend and colleague of B. F. Westcott and J. B. Lightfoot. Fellow of Trinity College, Cambridge, eminent New Testament scholar. His study, *The Way, the Truth and the Life*, is one of the outstanding works of nineteenth-century English theology.

12 **David Gwenallt Jones** (1899–1969). Welsh poet, critic and scholar. After a Marxist period he became an Anglican for a time, but eventually returned to the Methodist tradition in which he grew up.

13 **John Keble** (1792–1866). In Newman's words, 'the true and original author of the Oxford Movement'. Scholar, poet and saint. Fellow of Oriel College, Oxford, then vicar of Hursley near Winchester. One of the most attractive figures of his time.

14 **Thomas Ken** (1637–1711). Bishop of Bath and Wells, refused to take the oath of allegiance to William III in 1689. Hymn writer, preacher and saint.

15 **Alexander Knox** (1757–1831). Lay theologian, living in

Dublin, much influenced by John Wesley in his youth. Man of wide interests, well read in the Greek Fathers, precursor of the Oxford Movement.

16 **J. Saunders Lewis** (1893–   ). Greatest living Welsh writer. One of the founders of the Welsh National party. Poet, critic, scholar and dramatist. Roman Catholic since 1932.

17 **Edwin Muir** (1887–1959). Born in the Orkneys, lived and worked in Edinburgh, London and on the Continent. Poet and critic. Writer of a visionary quality whose true importance has not been recognized.

18 **John Henry Newman** (1800–1891). Theologian, preacher, poet. Leader of the Oxford Movement, converted to Roman Catholicism in 1845; became a member of the Oratory. Cardinal in 1879. One of the most outstanding of English theologians; precursor of Vatican II.

19 **Francis Paget** (1851–1911). Bishop of Oxford in 1901, having been a senior student and Dean of Christ Church. Contributor to the collection of essays, *Lux Mundi*, 1889. Scholar and pastor in the tradition of the Oxford Movement.

20 **Edward Bouverie Pusey** (1800–1882). Old Testament scholar, preacher and spiritual director. Professor and Canon of Christ Church, 1828–82. After Newman's conversion the unrivalled leader of the Catholic movement in the Church of England.

21 **Christopher Smart** (1722–71). Poet, some of whose finest work, e.g. *Jubilate Agno*, was written when he was confined in a lunatic asylum.

22 **Jeremy Taylor** (1613–67). Bishop of Down and Dromore in Northern Ireland. Preacher, writer and theologian. Outstanding representative of the Laudian school of Anglican theology.

23 **Herbert Thorndike** (1598–1672). Prebendary of Westminster, scholar and theologian. An unusually systematic and methodical theologian who greatly influenced some of the Tractarians.

24 **Thomas Traherne** (1638–74). Son of a Hereford shoemaker, vicar of Credenhill and chaplain to Sir Orlando Bridgman. Poet and prose writer of exceptional quality. His *Centuries of Meditations* was first published in 1908.

25 **Henry Vaughan** (1622–95). Welsh doctor living and practising near Brecon. Poet in the school of George Herbert; considered by many the most deeply mystical of the Anglican poets of his century.

26 **John and Charles Wesley** (1703–91), (1707–81). Brothers, priests of the Church of England, founders of the Methodist movement, the one by his preaching and organizing ability, the other by his hymns. Two of the greatest evangelists England has ever known.

27 **Brooke Foss Westcott** (1823–1901). Bishop of Durham, New Testament scholar and theologian, Fellow of Trinity College, Cambridge. With Lightfoot and Hort, assured that the critical methods of biblical scholarship should be used for and not against the Church's faith.

28 **William Wordsworth** (1770–1850). Greatest of the English romantic poets. In his youth strongly influenced by the French Revolution, increasingly conservative in his political and religious views as he grew older.

Index